DEAR OPRAH

CONFESSIONS OF A
MIDDLE-CLASS WHITE GIRL

Suzan Vaughn

Cover design: graphiction
Cover/interior silhouette art: Tom Neuman/WildWare
Interior silhouette clip art: Art Explosion/Nova Development

To my beautiful mother, Janice Audrey

Not a saint but an angel, and my own personal cheering section.
I love you more than words can say.

(Photo by Linn Felthaus)

CONTENTS

CONTENTS cont'd

PROLOGUE
An Open Letter to Oprah

Dear Oprah,

Millions of us love you - at least we think we do. We don't even really know you, although we do know a lot about you. We know that you are conscientious about your work, open about your life's challenges, and generous of heart.

You play big and are joyful as a result of monetary giving. We know you are a fearless interviewer, but also a flawed human being just like the rest of us, which gives us some comfort and a lot of hope. Our love is based on a good measure of fantasy too. How fun.

We see ourselves in you, and dream that we could be just as successful, even with our own flaws - that we are lovable even in our imperfection. We pretend you are our best listener, our closest friend, a woman with a good ear and a wise tongue.

I've undertaken this book on the premise that you, best fantasy friend to millions, will hear my confessions. Just as many have felt compelled to confess on the sets of your television shows, I am in the confessional here.

Shopping around the title to this book taught me that not everyone loves you, Oprah, and in some ways that gave me great comfort. You learned to stand tall against any judgments hurled at you, continuing to move forward brilliantly.

You have changed television for the better with positive and innovative programming.

I confess: I like the medium. You really do have the best producers in the business and I admire that. And now I love not only your shows but also the Oprah Winfrey Network (OWN). I even upgraded to a premium cable TV package to be in your company again, making a financial investment in OWN.

I am paying for insights, inspiration, and personal growth, and I have not been disappointed. OWN offers programming that motivates, uplifts, and helps viewers (now participants) to live our best lives. We are taught to own our talents, own ourselves as spiritual beings, and own our magnificence.

My psychological health has been served, so the investment is a good one even though my insurance company doesn't have a category for claims related to a higher cable bill due to TV mental health tune-ups. But wait! There's more!

As a bonus and as a result of OWN and "The Oprah Winfrey Show," I am able to commune with regular, interesting, accomplished, stimulating black individuals missing from my daily world. I appreciate that about all black producers, OWN being the biggest and best.

The network offers new life to the American vocabulary, unavailable before this decade, adding black dialects and ways of being in the world to our common dialogue. Although I, along with other white folks, still struggle to figure out what is politically correct in our world today, our arms are open.

I saw a Tyler Perry interview on OWN yesterday. OMGoddess! What a wonderful glimpse into this great man/woman (Madea!). He's just one of the gifted black people at OWN giving me a window into another world view and I'm grateful to be educated as a result.

The more I look, the more I'm allowed in, the more I know more deeply that we are all the same at the core, regardless of race. We are the race of humanity. I always knew that intellectually, but your interviews have clarified my vision.

I was in Heaven getting to know the likes of actors Michael B. Jordan, Chiwetel Ejiofor, and Idris Elba. To see into the hearts and minds of young, strong, capable, thoughtful black men is a gift some of us can't find any other way.

In his interview, Jordan says that movies like "Fruitvale Station" show producers that a wider audience is interested in the black experience.

I overheard two white women talking about "12 Years A Slave" just before it came out at the theater.

"I heard it's very violent," the first woman said.

"Well, I won't be seeing it then," said her friend.

But I could hardly wait to see the film.

While I understand shrinking from violence, it's more important for me to see and face our history and confront our cruelty. Otherwise, I would find it hard to believe what people are capable of doing to their fellow humans.

Seeing these realistic historical movies makes me a more educated person. I've been deepened and become more compassionate as a result of stories of the human spirit that I've viewed on the silver screen.

I'm also the first one in line to put my money down for movies like Lee Daniel's "The Butler," "42," "Jungle Fever," "The Help," "The Secret Life of Bees," "The Color Purple," any Tyler Perry movie, and other films that highlight black life then and now.

The confessions in this book are real. They're secrets about life choices, mistakes, victories, triumphs, rejections, healing, and private encounters with race, love, surrender, and redemption.

These are secrets millions of us might share with you if we had an opportunity to sit on your couch.

May you be blessed in all you do, sister-friend,

Suzan Vaughn
San Luis Obispo, California
June 2014

ONE

THE OPRAH FACTOR

The whole point of being alive is to evolve into the complete person you were intended to be.

~ Oprah Winfrey

THE WORLD'S CONFIDANTE

An Academy Award nomination is a pretty big event in the life of an actor, but Jonah Hill, nominated for his supporting role in "Moneyball," said the greatest thing that had ever happened to him was sitting down with Oprah. Wow.

Liz Lemon, Tina Fey's character on the TV show "30 Rock," "worships at the church of Oprah" and confesses her deepest, darkest secret to Oprah: Liz kissed a girl who then drowned, and she's afraid she's somehow responsible for the girl's death. The skit is part of the show, but it illustrates what you mean to millions of people.

Oprah is our fantasy priestess where we can come to vent, and where it will be okay, because she has confessed her own sins to us. Is that it? Is that what creates a craving for her ear? Is it that she has laid herself bare to us, so we feel safe telling her what we judge ourselves about most harshly? Is it that we know she'll understand because even though she is *all that*, she is also only human?

When Miss Robbie, star of "Welcome to Sweetie Pie's," and former back-up songstress for Ike and Tina Turner, hosted Oprah at her St. Louis soul food restaurant, she confessed, "When I grow up, I wanna be like Oprah." The woman is in her 70s.

"I admire Oprah because she's a black woman who has struggled and made it," Miss Robbie said. "It was really exciting to meet

Oprah. I mean, when she was in the restaurant, I felt like I was on top of the world." Now that's a legacy I admire. Oh yeah. I want people to feel on top of the world in my presence. Wonder if it requires fame.

Julianne Hing of *ColorLines* magazine wonders in the magazine's blog how much of Oprah's appeal comes from the fact that she embodies women's worst insecurities about themselves. She admits that she's not a fan, but gives Oprah her proper due for cultivating an intimacy with her audience, revolutionizing 20th century media, and being a brave, charismatic, and powerful woman of color.

She and I are both inspired by some of the same things Oprah has done.

"I love seeing the elaborate surprises Oprah plans for everyday people, the way she orchestrates tearful reunions and 24-hour makeovers and swoops in like an actual angel to make people's dreams come true. It is crazy-making entertainment," Hing writes.

"I believe, even on my meanest days, that Oprah's quest for global dominance is fueled at least in part by a desire to do some good. And I do believe that she is committed to empowering women and girls, that she wants to give people hope and encourage folks to wake up to the power we all have to make change in the world. So I consume the media she creates even when I'm uncertain if I can stomach more of her self-absorption and moralizing. I am electrified and enraged by Oprah.

"I could not turn away from her even if I bothered to try," Hing states.

Well, while I don't presume that Oprah is "questing for global dominance," I did think Hing had a few interesting points.

Margie Barron, a writer for the *Tolucan Times* in Toluca Lake,

Calif., calls you a sincere and gracious lady. "Maybe that's why everybody loves Oprah," she writes.

But for me, her seeming inability to be anything other than what she really is, and the sincerity and genuine openness of her interviews, is where I believe the magic lies.

Oprah's candid personal style creates an intimate ambiance for her guests, both on the stage and in the audience. It is as if we are all close friends, getting to know the people we've wondered about, wanted to get to know.

Some of the biggest celebrities in the world have opened up about their painful pasts, admitted their flaws, laughed about their pleasures, and offered up their demons. And it's partly because Oprah has confided in us, sharing her own life story of sexual abuse, weight struggles, philanthropic joys, and beliefs about how things are in our world. She reveals her own secrets and enables her guests to reveal theirs.

For most of us, it's hard to imagine a long line of journalists, day after day, waiting for an interview, some asking truly stupid questions. But Margie Barron did understand:

"Seeing her at the interview session, Oprah was everything I expected her to be, and my expectations were very high. I expected her to be pleasant and inspirational, and she was. I expected her to be generous, and she was. Not with a car or other lavish gifts that have surprised her audience members over the years, but she was generous with her time and thoughtful answers to the questions she got from the TV writers."

Thinking how hard it must be to maintain that perfect persona, Barron says she asked if Oprah ever felt like taking a day off from being Oprah.

"Wearing the color purple," writes Barron, "the 56-year-old talk show queen answered me as if I were an old friend concerned with her well-being: 'Yes, many times. I have felt the same as everybody. The difference is I have a TV show and I don't have a substitute host. I have to show up even when I'm not feeling 100 percent. Sometimes I'll come out and they [the audience] say, 'You look tired.' 'I am tired, people,' she sighs at the thought of those exhausting days."

Like the rest of her adoring audience, I see myself in her. Like Oprah, I've struggled with weight, addiction, and self-hatred. Like her, I left a job in broadcast journalism, scared to death to give up that $20,000 a year, but dying a slow death in the newsroom, shackled to the telling of the darkest news of the day. But through her, I vicariously live my dream of the joy the tender concern of being a great philanthropist brings.

Through Oprah, I rejoiced in her giving when she offered the many wrapped and personally named Christmas gifts to orphans in Africa. I thrilled with her when teachers in her audience who needed a car received one. I celebrated with her when the young black men from Howard University marched in, paying tribute on her next to last "Oprah Show." I marveled at her when she spoke directly to us, her audience, on her very last "Oprah Show," her words touching my heart as I related. That's exactly how I felt about my own talk show audience, and the one thing that kept me going in the sometimes-brutal broadcasting world.

I'm also pretty sure that all of her accomplishments barely compare to the greatest gift of all she shared with us: reuniting with her beloved sister, Patricia. We can understand what it means to be her, finding a person who wants nothing more than her love and kinship. I have a sister like that too.

Oprah's a real, live phenomenal woman. The time, personal work, and down and dirty dedication it takes to be where she is, is thought-provoking. It puts her right on the Maya Angelou list of phenomenal women who have sought to surround themselves with people who could still be honest with them.

We love Oprah for so many reasons. She makes us laugh too. When Madea meets Sophia on the road for the OWN promo, I was so glad I didn't have to "check with my cable provider" to find the OWN channel on my own cable system – otherwise I would have missed the funniest promo ever produced for television. *Hellerrr!*

TWO

PARTING THE VEIL
ON ANOTHER WORLD

"Up until then I'd thought that white people and colored people getting along was the big aim, but after that I decided everybody being colorless together was a better plan. I thought of that policeman, Eddie Hazelwurst, saying I'd lowered myself to be in this house of colored women, and for the very life of me I couldn't understand how it had turned out this way, how colored women had become the lowest ones on the totem pole. You only had to look at them to see how special they were, like hidden royalty among us."

~ Lily, in *The Secret Life of Bees,* by Sue Monk Kidd

NEW ORLEANS STYLE AT THE TROLLEY STOP CAFÉ

I have a craving for black culture, and in the winter of 2012 I make my first trip to New Orleans with a friend. I know that in the Big Easy, African, Native American, and European history is blended to create a spicy cultural soup that will satisfy my longing.

Breakfast is served at the Trolley Stop Café. As I look over the menu, I'm at a loss to find a breakfast with fewer than about 3,000 carbohydrate-laced calories. Settling on three dollar-sized pancakes, a scrambled egg, and two slices of bacon as the least of many Southern food evils, I shoot a sideways glance at the man and woman seated slightly behind my left shoulder.

The table for four is just right for this couple, who are eating from big plates of fried fish, fried chicken, and fried potatoes. The food reminds me that Southern chef Paula Deen has been diagnosed on this day with Type 2 diabetes and it's only 10 o'clock in the morning.

(Of course the bodacious and lovable Deen will attempt to roll her illness into a plum marketing opportunity by becoming a spokesperson for a proper diabetic diet in the weeks that follow, Goddess love her: she, who got where she is by, in her words, "workin' like a dayum dawg." But she is stopped by a 2013 videotaped deposition where she admits to using the n-word in her past. The 66-year-old Southerner was subsequently fired by the Food Network and lost multiple endorsements before beginning to remake her brand.)

Our Trolley Stop waitress, however, has always had a hard life. I can tell. She serves this food but she doesn't eat it. After serving it to customers for hours, she's probably uninterested in any food. My guess is she'd rather have a cigarette. I have to ask her name – Angie – since she's the type of woman who I'm sure told the boss she wasn't wearing her damn name on a clothing tab. *"People can ask if they want to know,"* I bet she told him.

I can see it's just another day for her, and here I am all excited. It's controlled, but Angie can feel it and it makes her take a step back emotionally. She's a black woman with an attitude but mouths to feed, so she relies on my tourist dollars. She *has* to be somewhat nice to me, a big blonde tourist from who knows where. But I consider it real and honest when she calls me "dahlin'," and I melt like butter in her hands.

I'm so happy to be here it's contagious, and although Angie is suspicious, she can't easily dismiss this particular blue-eyed Yankee. Somewhere in her, in the place where we are one, she can feel me, even though I'm a little too eager to please her. A lifetime of living in a white world has left me with a yearning for African Americans, as well as a fear of saying or doing the wrong thing in their company.

Is it attributable to past or parallel lifetimes? Strong urges and feelings in this life are well explained by that, and one strong desire I have is to rest my head like a young child against a very large black woman's breast.

There's no doubt in my mind that I've been in that position at some time somewhere. I've had that happy, close, and loving memory since I can remember. When the movie "The Help" came out, I saw more clearly where it might have come from as we all glimpsed the hearts of those mostly black women who cared for other people's children at the expense of their own.

I try to order the special, but Angie tells me it's over.

"Too late, baby," she says. I smile, and melt a little more because a black woman has called me "baby." I make another menu choice that meets with her approval.

Angie heads for the kitchen to hang the order. This woman's sanction is hard to come by, so it feels like a small victory for an old longing to please her and to express my appreciation for her race.

Later we're having dinner in a very nice restaurant. Like many of the workforce that relies on tips here, our efficient and pleasant 25-year-old blonde waitress calls us "ma'am." A young black man, about her age, with impeccable grooming, assists Blondie. He has perfectly bright white teeth with beautiful full lips, close-cut hair, a red tie, a black vest, and starched, rolled-up shirtsleeves. His server fashion is topped off with a black apron over dress slacks. This boy cuts an image. It's too irresistible not to say something.

Raising my hand in the air in his direction I say, "Excuse me."

"Yes, ma'am?" he says, approaching the table.

"Did you know that every woman loves a sharp-dressed man?" I ask him.

He laughs. "I'd have to say I'm kind of aware of that," he grins.

My companion and I reiterate that we just want him to know it's definitely working for him. He does. It's still nice to hear, and we hope to start off his work night well, but take no further action as neither of us are cougars – we just appreciate beauty and class in a young one. But I bet he's met some real cougars, right there in that nice restaurant, just because of how graciously he accepted my compliment and how skillfully he retreated.

By complimenting Will the waiter, I'm also following a vow I work at keeping: never withhold a compliment hanging on my tongue. Unlike our Trolley Stop server, Angie, who is not at all comfortable with that kind of talk, the young man takes it lightly with the understanding that it makes economic sense for him. Plus, when you look like he does, you learn a thing or two about getting away cleanly.

But you could tell Angie was reserved about anyone invading her space or of unexpected rewards. My guess is that the latter came with a heavy price in her young life, and the memories sit like stones in her belly now, 50 years later.

"Thank you for your good service," I told her after breakfast, as I pressed a 30-percent tip into her hand on my way out. She stammered out a thank you, taken aback at my searching her out instead of leaving it on the table.

LIVING WATERS CHURCH

Over the years, I've searched for acceptable ways to serve my wish to learn about black culture. The Living Waters Church was one of those ways.

A very large auditorium-type church, this place rocks with traditional hymns and choirs, and the sing-song ministry from the pulpit was powerful. Ladies with beautiful Sunday hats met me at the door, welcoming me by pressing a program in my hand. And just beyond those double doors an astonishing sight: more than 100 black people, or at least all shades of coffee, right in my own white-bread community. A large part of our three percent, right there in one place!

It was thrilling until the sermon was given. By the end of it, I felt so beaten up by the pointing out of my shortcomings and the portrayal of a wrathful Creator that I couldn't go back. I wanted to shake them into a positive message of love and redemption. *Black folks don't need to be further beaten up,* I told myself. But instead, I just stayed away.

After my trip to Living Waters, I saw a woman I recognized from there waiting to be served at a local deli. I smiled at her from 15 feet away. She avoided my gaze. I knew she couldn't fathom why I would want to engage her, and she didn't see that my smile was for her. She couldn't see it.

I've had the same experience with many other black people too. My smile sends them into hiding. Never mind even thinking about approaching them.

Gotta be careful. Whitey can't be trusted. Is that what was going on here? If it was, it makes even more sense as to why we love you so much, Oprah. You allow us to love you: a black woman who lets us in completely. When others aren't available or can't take it in, you represent your race and we send our affection to you.

But now that we have a black president, maybe things are changing.

YOU KNOW I WANT TO BE PC

Which brings me to: What terms can I use without offending? I want to be "politically correct" when it comes to expressing myself about folks who are other-than-my-own-race, and I'm afraid.

A LESSON FROM MAYA ANGELOU

When I'm wondering about whether my words will be PC, I think of whether they would have gotten me kicked out of Maya Angelou's house. That happened to someone who made a racist remark in her home, and she documented it in one of her books. He got booted out, and I trembled at the thought.

I can only hope that, as the professor she was, she'd educate me if I screwed up instead of showing me the door, but this is how I measure my words and thoughts about using appropriate language: Would Maya Angelou have approved? And do the words from my mouth please the Divine?

During one interview with Oprah, Dr. Angelou stated that you should never allow anybody to say anything negative about anyone in your home.

Oprah responded by saying she had seen Dr. Angelou, without any embarrassment, make people leave the house for telling a racist joke.

Dr. Angelou nodded, stating that negative statements are like poison, creating sounds and images that fill the air like bats. They can take you over, she explained to Oprah, and remain in your house, your mind, and your life. So whenever she'd heard a rude or hateful thing said, she'd send the person who said it away.

The spirit of this truly phenomenal woman, poet, and interpreter of the black experience will never leave us. Over five decades she wrote more than 35 books, and at 86 deserved a deep and peaceful rest. May she enjoy a warm welcome in her new and non-physical home.

QUESTIONS

It is 2013, and the OWN network has put out a call over the internet to anyone who wants to wish Dr. Angelou a happy 85th birthday. I can't resist. I become a part of the sea of well-wishers for this phenomenal woman. But I still struggle with my words, wanting them to be PC.

I want to write about how I so admire her. But is it okay to refer to her race? She's so much more than that, but her heritage is such a part of what makes her who she is. Is it more PC to just express my gratitude for her example as an admirable woman, and leave her race out of it altogether? If I do, I feel as if I am leaving out all that it means that she is black, that she is coming from a race of people who are strong survivors, that she beat back hatred, prejudice, threats, and fear to rise.

She learned to listen so well during her childhood years of being mute, that later every word she expressed was wise and thoughtfully measured. And for this, for what she had fought for, for who she had been and who she became, and for her blackness too, she will always be a national treasure.

Maya Angelou was also one of the remarkable African Americans who led the way to a black president.

And would it be PC to say, "Hey, he's half white. I can claim him too"? Or would that discount the wonderful accomplishment of electing our first black president?

Comedian Wanda Sykes says, "I'm gonna call him half white if he screws up." Fair enough. Wanda's one of those sisters who helps me get a black perspective on life. She has a white wife and two white kids. She says if she really wants to mess with people, she'll push her wife out of the way and take off with the stroller full of two little white twins. Really gets people going. No doubt, Wanda. I just love her. And what's more, I get it (as much as a white person can).

White girls like me barely exposed to any black folks have to get information from people like Wanda Sykes, Nene Leaks, Omarosa, Robbie Montgomery, Madea, and Oprah. I love to see that affluent black folks are getting face time on TV.

I'm grateful for the education.

THE AFRICAN QUEEN

A woman with skin the color of strong black coffee looked back at me from the audience. Smiling with lips closed, perfectly serene, her face was that of a woman who had survived adversity and found peace on the other side. I drew strength from her during my talk, and okay, I admit it, I was excited about the possibility of giving her a hug.

Now, *puhleeze*. This was not a sexual thing. It was partly my interest in African Americans and partly the beauty and grace of this African Queen. The love and peace coming from this woman drew me to her. Her face was very round, with red cheeks, big dark doe eyes, and full, smiling lips. I can only guess at her age, because age is so subjective for me. I am much more in tune with energetic age. But she was between 30 and 50.

During the service at the Church of the Comforter in Santa Barbara, two experienced psychics offered messages to the audience. Reverend Judy asked the African Queen if she would like to get a message. The Rev brought through the picture of a man. And, oh boy, I sure saw him clearly too. He looked like an African prince. He wore beautifully colored robes and a showy headpiece. The African Queen's serenity fit right in there under his arm. But I also felt that the relationship would not be without challenges.

Soon, it was my turn to speak. Picking out a few responsive faces I could deliver to, hers was the middle anchor in the room. She sat in the second row center, fully there for the talk called "Animal Death: A Spiritual Journey."

At service's end, several people formed a line to talk to me. My intention is to be fully present for each person, but one lady is bending my ear a little longer than I'm comfortable with and I'm still learning the grace of moving to the next person. Anxiety rises because I want to speak to the African Queen before she leaves, so I look for an opening to wrap it up with my talkative fan and move on, lest the Queen get away. Noting the hint of desperation in myself, I surrender the event to my Higher Sources.

If I am meant to hug this sister-friend, please make it so, I pray.

She seems to be chatting with church folks, checking out leaflets, and taking her time, and I wonder: *Does she feel a connection too?*

Finally, there is a break in the line and she is still there. My smile lights up and I approach her with both of my arms stretched out. I'm comin' for her and she lets me in. As I embrace her I say, "Hello, my sister. I recognize you. I don't know where it's coming from, but I do."

She says, "I do too."

I tell her, "In your reading, I saw the strong African man too, and he looked very princely."

She smiles a little more and asks, "Did you? Hmmm."

It's a warm connection and I feel complete with it as she slips out the door, her lips closed but turned up slightly at the corners in a smile of pensive contentment.

MARVELOUS MABEL

In the only photograph I have of her, Mabel's eyes shine warmly from her oval face. Her dark skin is smooth and her smile is sweet. A deep love for her overcomes me each time I look at the old photo.

It's hard to tell, but in the photograph Mabel is probably in her 60s, standing on the porch with my white ancestors and holding a baby, my eldest cousin. She was a Godsend to a family of five young kids who had just lost their saintly mother. The youngest, a girl, was the toddler in Mabel's arms in the photo. The oldest, a boy, was 15.

Mable had two or three kids and a husband of her own. At harvest time, her young boys worked at the farm when there was work to be had. She walked to work, a mile or two. Her husband was the boss of a maintenance crew.

Mable became part of the family once Donia, my paternal grandmother, got sick and could no longer care for a house, a husband and five kids. Grandfather hired Mabel to take care of his wife and their kids while he went to the foundry every day, often for double shifts. Donia was being treated for pneumonia, but after she died an autopsy revealed that breast cancer had killed her.

Mabel stayed on to care for the farm, the house, the devastated widower, and the forlorn kids. She had help from the eldest daughter, my Aunt Mary, who was about 14, and all the kids pitched in to work the farm as best they could.

The family form of transportation was foot or mule, and Grandfather walked to the steel mills in Birmingham because he didn't have the dime to ride a streetcar. Once he received his paycheck, he took the streetcar now and then.

His eldest boy, Ken, remembers Mabel as a warm-hearted woman, like his mother. I asked him to remember Mabel for me when he had just turned 87 and he did.

"After I was out of the house, got married, and David was born, we lived in Texas. We were passing through to see all the family on our way to Savannah, where we would live for a good while. Mabel left word with one of my sisters that if I came through there I would have to get in touch so she could see her grandbaby. That was the last time we saw her," he remembered.

It would have been typical for Mabel to claim Ken's first-born as a grandchild. I wish I could have known her. Perhaps it was as a result of his young life being nurtured by Mabel that Ken was inspired to do so much missionary work in Africa, focusing on spending his labor, time, and money on building classrooms for educating children there.

My own dad remembered Mabel for her kindness too – and for saving one of his fingers!

At about the age of seven, Dad sliced his finger open clear to the tendon while cutting and harvesting wheat with a scythe-type knife. Mabel got some bootblack and sugar, mixed it with some other household substance, and stopped the bleeding. Until the day Dad died, he had a black vein running through the top of his pointer finger's last knuckle. He pointed to it more than once to tell me the story of Mabel, the first African American woman he ever loved.

WHITE PEOPLE ARE LOOKIN' AT YOU

Comedian Wanda Sykes is one of the people in my life who teaches me how it is to be black.

"White people are lookin' at you," she says, quoting the admonishments of her parents when she acted up, or, more likely, acted like a child when she was one.

This warning was supposed to motivate the kids to toe the line, straighten up, and quit doing whatever it was they were doing. In Wanda's case, it was chair dancing in the back seat of a car moving down the road.

She's produced a brilliant HBO video of a stand-up performance in Washington, D.C., that is side-splittingly hilarious. "I'ma Be Me" is its defiant name, and it gives me hope and inspiration in the area of throwing off the chains of needing approval and being anything less than fully authentic. Thanks, Wanda.

Now that we have a black president, Wanda says she can relax a little bit. Doesn't have to be so black all the time. Now, she's gonna throw a whole watermelon on her shoulder, tap dance, say f-you to Whitey, and go get some chicken at Popeyes!

"Gotta be dignified before. One wrong move sets back the whole race," she says.

Thank the Goddess I don't have my mascara on yet since I'm laughing my ass entirely off (LMAEO) from watching and listening to Wanda Sykes. Toni, a lesbian friend, shared Wanda's DVD with me. I share it with those who can appreciate it.

THREE

SEEING BENEATH THE SURFACE

There is no excellent beauty that hath not some strangeness in the proportion.

> ~ Francis Bacon, writer and philosopher,
> born 1561, London
>
> *paraphrased by writer/poet Edgar Allan Poe in "Ligeia"*

BREAKING STEREOTYPES

We are all striving for balance: emotional, mental, spiritual, and physical. I've lived for many years above the neck but as I face mid-life, I've grown more into my body, focusing on physical health and vitality, as well as emotional and spiritual peace.

I boast now to myself that I'm not prejudiced, so my Higher Sources decide to show me where my own personal prejudices are hiding. It works that way.

I've invited that kind of relationship where a mirror is held up to me for self-examination when I make such a self-declaration. But that doesn't mean it's a comfortable process.

Common prejudices for whites often involve African Americans, and I've commented how I've become aware of those in myself, and even learned to appreciate different kinds of black culture, in many ways thanks to you, Oprah.

But while my experience with African Americans is limited, I've always lived among, learned from, and befriended Mexicans and Mexican-Americans.

I know many people who resent growing Latino communities, but they have no understanding of Mexico's history with the States.

The truth is that the United States weaseled its way into taking California from the Mexicans by creating a false war, and Mexican descendants are taking it back here in the Golden State through sheer numbers.

The Mexican–American War (1846-47) aimed to expand American territories to the Pacific coast, a goal of President James K. Polk. As the U.S. and Mexico squabbled over ownership of the Texas territory, American forces occupied New Mexico and California, then invaded parts of Northern Mexico. The American army captured Mexico City, handing a victory to the United States.

As a consequence, Mexico was forced to sell the territories of Alta California and a large area comprising New Mexico, Arizona, Nevada, Utah, and parts of Wyoming and Colorado; admit that Texas was U.S. property; cite the Rio Grande as its national border; and accept $15 million as a fair price for the land. In the Treaty of Guadalupe Hidalgo, Mexicans in those annexed areas had the choice of relocating to Mexico or receiving American citizenship with full civil rights. More than 90 percent remained.

When I was growing up, I realize that when I saw a yard full of old, broken-down cars, I might have associated that with Mexican families – a stereotype I'm no longer comfortable with.

I began to ask myself what these families' lives might be like. Were the yard owners held down and held back because of their ethnicity? Was a family trying to make ends meet with a small business on the side that might bring in a few dollars? How much did my own upbringing contribute to my attitude?

What if these families were Anglo, had access to higher education, made some money, and put their cars on land hidden behind fences they could afford? We might call them clever or resourceful if they could resurrect an old car for a young family member. I've sold many a car to a Mexican family because fixing it would cost the value of the car and the man in the family or another family member could fix it.

My cousin Susan has several Mexican neighbors. When I was on a visit there, three of us struggled to get a large piece of furniture to the curb to put a "Free" sign on it.

As we work our way to the sidewalk, three neighbors, Mexican men, come right over to help. They wrestle the thing to the front yard with us, and Susan asks if they want the piece of furniture. They're happy to take it.

Back inside the house, we all wipe our foreheads and let out a sigh, when there is a knock on the door. It's one of the Mexican neighbors asking if we need help with any other moving. I'm astounded and confounded at their helpfulness that's way above and beyond the call of neighborliness.

Susan says her neighbors are always that helpful to her, knowing she has physical limitations. She says they look out for her.

In my college years I lived with lots of Mexican and Mexican-American neighbors. They loved to work hard and party hard on the weekends. Live music and lots of color were their hallmarks, and they were always gracious when I practiced my Spanish on them. But because their resources were limited, you could stand in line most of the weekend to get your clothes into the laundry we all shared. The Mexican folks were bringing in the laundry of everyone they knew.

Other family members have shared their experiences of Mexican men and women with me too. My brother Sam, a construction foreman, says whenever he is hunting for a crew to do a job, he chooses Mexican workers. I ask him about his choice.

"They are hard-working and there is no whining like you get from Anglo guys," he tells me.

My dad had experiences with our south-of-the-border neighbors too.

As a union leader for Pacific Bell, Dad served as president of the jurisdiction covering all of California, Nevada, Oregon, Washington, and part of Idaho.

One story Dad told me took place in the early 1960s.

Cesar Chavez, president of the National Farm Workers Association, came to visit and request support. Chavez wanted to have the short hoe declared illegal, so he asked leaders of the telephone union ORTT (Order of Repeatermen and Toll Testboardmen) to try out the hoe themselves. None could do the hoeing for more than 10 minutes because their backs became so sore from bending over.

Chavez received the support he requested.

As a union organizer, Dad fought for equal pay, workers' rights, and medical benefits, and against sexual harassment. By definition this included equal rights for all union members.

Finally, in my own life now, many of my Mexican-American friends bring forward not only their rich culture but are well-educated and brilliant, like my CPA, Lisa Gonzalez.

LOOKS AND LOOKERS

Making my way through my teens in the early and mid-1970s, beautiful people were pervasive in my world because I grew up within an hour's drive of Hollywood. There was a whole lot of plastic in the Hollywood Hills, not to mention in my own childhood home of beauty and its wiles, and gorgeous women and dapper men made me suspicious.

I saw the workings of physical beauty's currency firsthand, and I made some sweeping prejudicial decisions about people who appeared physically perfect or Hollywood glamorous.

For my own mother, beauty did not equate to happiness all the time, although she was always grateful for her good looks. In one striking photo she looks like a screen double for Liz Taylor.

The photo always draws me in closer each time I look at it. She is in her mid-30s, seated theatrically with three of her four daughters, wearing a blood-red dress ("I had a knock-out figure," she told me) and sporting perfectly long, tapered fingernails polished a matching color.

But what is striking is that she looks as miserable as I've ever seen her, and indeed she was.

The picture was taken only weeks before she married a man she did not love in exchange for financial help and security, crying all the way to the home of the justice of the peace. The ceremony itself would set the stage for this particular marriage, when the justice came in from the garden, shoes encrusted with mud, threw on his robe, and performed the marriage ceremony carelessly, much to my mother's disgust.

My prejudice against the ultra-lovely still rises as a sour taste in my mouth. I fight against negative thoughts that beautiful people are less developed intellectually and emotionally, although perhaps better trained in the art of manipulation.

Even as I confess to my bias against those who are unreasonably physically attractive, I know they've got a set of problems all their own.

I hope you don't mind me saying so, O, but you and I are blessed with physical beauty that is, on a scale of one to 10, neither a one nor a 10. Although at times we are both very attractive women, I don't think "drop-dead gorgeous" is a fitting description of either of us.

And if there's one thing I know for sure, being a 10 on the raving-beauty end of the scale seems to be more problematic than it's worth. We're lucky not to be on either extreme.

What I want to say about the beautiful people is: Don't hate them, because extreme beauty comes with a lot of heartbreak, peril, and challenges that being within the normal range of beauty doesn't.

My friend Dee, for example, is a tall drink of hot chocolate. An actor and model, he's blessed and cursed with some of the most beautiful good looks I've personally ogled. I'm sympathetic to the poor baby, who is so handsome he told me at times he craves a full body condom as a defense against lascivious looks from his admirers.

AN INTELLIGENT WOMAN UNRECOGNIZED

I've been examining the effects of physical beauty for a long time. In the mid-1990s, I experienced such a strong emotional reaction to an experience in a radio station where I worked that I was compelled to analyze it carefully.

My three-hour morning newscast had just ended and my hour-long talk show was about to begin. It was 9 a.m. and at 9:05 my talk-show guest needed to be in her place in the studio. Passing the sales and production departments, I escorted the woman from the lobby into the studio, settling in for an interview about the good work a local non-profit organization she was affiliated with was doing.

She was stunning. Her ivory-skinned face was flawless. She had huge green eyes with long black lashes, and her face was framed by long, lovely, thick and slightly wavy black hair.

Inside the radio station, her passage through the offices en route to the live studio had made news throughout the building. Every male employee in the place was casually finding an excuse to slip past the studio window and have a look. Just like in the movies, the stooges' buffoonery went as far as actually running into each other from not looking where they were going. I watched the comedy unfold through sideways glances out the studio window between questions to my guest.

She was an excellent spokesperson, knowing when to answer, when to listen, when to expound, and how long to talk. The woman had a lot more going for her than just how she looked, but the male employees were oblivious to her words and her intellect.

At the conclusion of the show, when she came out of the studio, my boss, the general manager, was there in a New York second, complimenting her on what a great job she'd done. His motives were transparent, flattering her and practically drooling over her in the most disgusting way. Later on, I found out he had no understanding of her subject matter.

His behavior made me cringe. I felt a wave of nausea wash over me. Wow! My body was having a very strong reaction. So I followed the normal path I follow when hit by an emotional Mack truck: I take a closer look.

It was a significant moment in realizing that I felt I didn't, and might never, measure up in the looks department. The nausea wasn't all about that, though. It was about the woman being valued so blatantly for her physical self *alone*.

I had made it imperative that people work harder to find out who I was. They had to look behind my physical appearance if they wanted to know me. I know now it wasn't a good strategy and I was fooling myself, but I felt my extra weight required people to relate to me on a level other than physical. The rebel in me, the way I grew up with food, my addictive nature – all these expanded my struggles with excess weight. My deeper self conspired to keep the pounds on so that men and women would approach me on a more intellectual level.

It was partly a reaction to my mother's life choices. Her looks had always been her currency and – I thought – a ruse. But that was the MO for women in the 1940s and 1950s, and it still persists today. Women were supposed to offer good looks, and men were supposed to bring money and security to a relationship, still a common trade-off today.

I was also reminded of a time when I lost a lot of weight, looked good, and was dropped by female friends who got worried about their husbands' wandering eyes.

It's not true that you can never be too rich, too thin, or too classically beautiful. You can indeed be over the top in any of those states of being. Or at least being the extreme in any of those areas can become a big problem.

Facing the challenge of continual unwanted attention, it's only natural for some people to retaliate against the superficial desires of others by using that power to their own benefit. Good looks are powerful door-openers and money-makers.

At its worst, beauty translates into a personality that takes and uses. Men especially are very willing to serve, own, and keep a beautiful woman. When men adore her as a goddess, I suspect it can be challenging for her to become a gracious giver.

BECKY

My sister Becky is an attractive redhead. Her flaming locks were the reason for her nickname, "Foxie." Somewhere in the 1960s, calling a woman "a fox" – or a higher compliment yet, "a *stone fox*" – meant she was physically beautiful. Since Becky did not fit the traditional waif model stereotype (as suggested by her era's supermodel, Twiggy), she felt it necessary to explain her nickname whenever it was used by anyone.

"I'm called 'Foxie' because of my red hair," she'd say. She didn't want people to think she was conceited or thought herself better than others, which is why she told people we didn't know well why we called her by that nickname.

Beauty comes with other challenges. When one is strikingly attractive, depth of relationship is difficult to achieve. Beautiful women and handsome men are sought after as objects, and it's hard to shake that.

JANENE

My sister Janene looks like the movie star Michelle Pfeiffer but that hasn't made her life much easier. She experienced a father who nearly killed her for crying as an infant, abusive relationships, and a parade of male admirers who wanted just one thing. Even when she chose a relationship with a man for his depth of wisdom, her beauty made him insecure about her loyalty to the relationship.

I asked her to comment on beauty for this book.

"What price have you paid for being beautiful?" I asked.

"About $8K for a face lift," she said jokingly, then went on to explain more seriously:

"I don't mind getting older. I'm not even afraid of death, but I don't want to age. I don't want to look like Joan Rivers or Cher. I will try to look my best until I am dead. And that depends on the amount of money I have to spend on anti-aging treatments or for how long I really care.

"I think a beautiful woman becomes a test for many men," Janene said, "almost as a hunter would view prey. The dynamics between men and beautiful women are complex and deep: When a man becomes obsessed by a beautiful woman, it gives her a lot of power.

"When I was dating, I found that *most* older men were looking for something they couldn't have again, which was a woman to make them feel the way their high school girlfriend used to. They don't want to give up that ever-elusive chase.

"After I divorced I thought it would be cool to date older men, because I thought they would've gotten much wiser and more insightful by now. Wrong! They are still mostly immature, only now it is more complicated for them. They wander around looking for a woman who will bring back their youth, forgetting that no other person will ever be able to make them 18 years old again.

"I suspect that almost any man over the age of 40 would pick a much younger woman if he could. You seldom see a wealthy man with a woman his own age at his side. And I would guess that at some point in a man's life, almost any younger woman looks beautiful, as long as she is young.

"I can only relate to being sought after as an object from before getting married.

I remember my boss at Kresge's drugstore encouraging me to meet him in the warehouse. He would then kiss and fondle me. It was my first job. I was so naive and confused about appropriate behavior that I allowed it. I didn't want to lose my job.

"A gorgeous woman with maturity and discrimination could be a formidable energy," she concluded.

MY MOTHER

Janene was taught by our mother that it's much better to be beautiful than the alternative. Mom taught her girls that it's better to be the one who is sought after than the one in a relationship that is deeply in love. The one who loves more is vulnerable. Though Mom doesn't consider herself a 'raving beauty,' beauty has been her calling card.

I'm not judging. I got the same message from Mom loud and clear: Physical attractiveness is the way, the truth, and the light. It was often difficult to realize I was not measuring up to the high standards of 18-inch waists and long, fluttering eyelashes. That's not to say that if I were ever to get the funds, you wouldn't find me in the nip-and-tuck chair, and right quick. Hey, I was raised that way.

Because of my mother's resemblance to Elizabeth Taylor, in her young years she fought off lascivious uncles, bosses, acquaintances, and boyfriends many a time. Just one of those times was in San Francisco.

"I was hungry, so I found this job in a mom-and-pop restaurant," she told me. "The owner was this big Greek guy, Dimitriov. He looked me over so I knew I was in trouble. 'You want a job?' he asked me. I said yes so he asked me what size I was for a uniform. He held one up and it was close to my size, a 10, and he told me to try it on and see if it fit.

"Just as I was getting into it he opened the door and came back in. That a**h*** ran his hand all the way up my dress! I was about 17, and I really needed the job, so I was just sick about it. Dimitriov's wife came into the room just as it happened, but she turned around and walked away. I had the job for about a week and then Dimitriov told me that his wife said to fire me. I was devastated," she remembered.

My mother had one small child and herself to feed at the time, so she was forced to look for work again. This scene repeated itself over her early work career more than once. In the eyes of the law, she was unprotected and even blamed.

ME

For most of my life, I have struggled with excess weight. I used food as a drug to numb difficult emotions when they surfaced.

At the height of my weight struggle, when I found myself about 160 pounds overweight, I traveled to South America. The people were very small Mayan descendants, and I was quite embarrassed trying to share a seat on the bus with one woman. It was evident as people jockeyed for position that they were all trying to avoid sitting next to the gigantic American woman.

It wasn't much better once I got home from my travels.

Boarding the tram to get from the international terminal to the commuter terminal, I struggled to get my suitcases on board the bus. The American men on the bus seemed frozen in their seats.

But years later when I had lost weight and was a normal size, I traveled again. The contrast was striking when several men offered to help me get my luggage on board that very same commuter bus.

BEAUTIFUL BABY

Beauty can sometimes kill the spirit, beginning in childhood.

Being classically attractive was not all it was cracked up to be for a baby blonde I know. Her beauty came with an extremely high price. I'll call her Helen.

At the young age of five or six, Helen's parents decided to take a trip. They left her in the care of a couple who shared their spiritual path, feeling assured that their child would be safe with this man and woman of God.

But the husband was not safe. He told this five-year-old that she was so beautiful he could not help himself – he had to have his hands and other parts of his adult body all over her. It was her fault that he had to molest her.

By the time Helen was a teenager, she was intent on destroying that same beauty with self-mutilation, drugs, and alcohol. She hated her good looks.

WHAT'S MOST IMPORTANT

Thank you, Oprah, for discussing physical beauty on many of your shows. As always, your programs helped me gain more clarity.

All the studies and statistics that have been conducted to date support the notion that it's the people in the balanced middle – not too beautiful and not too homely, not too rich and not too poor, not too thin and not too fat – who are the ones with the best chance at contentment, the end goal.

And finally, no matter what our looks, the inevitable process of aging has its own effects.

I've seen a few little traces of age on your face lately, Oprah, as you turn 60. They are more like subtle shadows that haven't been there before, hidden by the hand of expert make-up artist Reggie Wells. I find them charming.

Inspired by you and women like Maya Angelou, I'm proud to have made it this far.

But what's most important to me now is understanding others, whatever their physical beauty or age. My highest calling has become to clear myself of generalized misjudgments, seeing the soul instead of the body.

SADIE FILES SUIT

When the jury summons arrived in the mail, I knew I wanted to serve. It was a good time for it in my life, and I was game, even though I had no idea of the subject matter. I've always been interested in the law and a chance to see it up close and personal was thrilling.

I reported promptly at 8:30 a.m. and the smooth ride and arrival at the courthouse made me aware that I was in the flow of things.

The San Luis Obispo County Courthouse is a beautiful building, now with security screening just like that of big cities. I laid my bag and books in the buckets and breezed through the metal detectors.

I was being considered by the court, prosecutors, defendants, and plaintiffs as a potential juror: one part of a group of 12 people who would decide what was right and true. Twelve people who would be affecting dozens of lives with our decision.

Television shows and films about the law – how it is administered, how juries perform, the thoughts I've had on how to responsibly vote for judges, the articles I've written on the same subject, and the talk shows I've hosted on all these topics – have kept my interest in law and all things legal alive and active. Now I had manifested a potential opportunity to serve, to watch, and to learn up close.

Each group of jury candidates was told that the case was about sexual harassment and wrongful termination but that was about it. As the process of *voir dire* began, potential jurors were asked a series of questions related to their experience of sexual harassment in the workplace. When it came my turn, I knew two things. I had to be completely honest, and that probably meant I'd be going home. Bummer.

After a series of acceptances and rejections of different juror candidates, it was my turn.

"Ms. Vaughn," said the prosecutor, "have you ever experienced sexual harassment in the workplace?"

"Yes," I replied, "on many occasions."

"Can you please tell the court the nature of your experiences?" he asked.

"I worked for 10 years at a local radio station. On more than one occasion, my boss told me that women were totally useless in any position other than prone and wondered aloud why any of us ever stood on our feet," I said. "He often made remarks about women being good only as sexual objects. Most of the time these comments were delivered in a joking manner, but we all knew he felt that way to some extent because of other remarks he made."

"What else happened there?" the prosecutor asked.

"I found myself reluctant to hire any applicants who were young, beautiful women because his behavior was so inappropriate I felt it could open the company up to a lawsuit," I said.

"Have you experienced any other forms of sexual harassment?" the prosecutor continued.

"I believe so, although it might be more appropriate to call it wrongful termination."

"Go on," he encouraged.

"When I was 27, I worked at a radio station in Lake Tahoe, where I found out later that the boss had hired me because he wanted to see if he could get me to have sex with him. Eventually, we did date. When the relationship ended, he stripped me of my duties one at a time, then fired me, saying I was not earning my salary," I told the court.

"Did you see an attorney?" the prosecutor asked.

"Yes," I said.

"What happened?"

"The attorney told me there was no money in it since I didn't make much, and that no lawyer would likely take the case," I reported.

"Thank you," the prosecutor said, turning to the judge. "We accept this juror." And the defense attorney nodded in agreement.

I was stunned, sure that my testimony would disqualify me. But I was also delighted to be a juror and looked forward to seeing the system at work.

Once behind closed doors, I lobbied for the job as presiding juror and won. (Don't think I didn't have a private chuckle about the fact that I, a pet psychic, was the presiding juror. 'Only in California,' I said to myself.)

The plaintiff was an attractive young blonde who claimed that two of the doctors within the group of doctors she had worked for were sexual harassers. She detailed their leering glances on a couple of occasions and a few inappropriate remarks. Her side tried to make a big deal about a time when one of the doctors came to her house to dress a wound. They also brought up a car ride to a conference where something probably happened between them, but mostly flirting is what it seemed like.

When the plaintiff took the stand, she was a terrible witness. Full of hostility and anger, she was unable to say how she had actually been hurt by the events physically, psychologically, financially or even emotionally. And even if every detail she recounted had been true, the incidences she reported were so wimpy in comparison to what most of us on the jury had experienced in the workplace, she seemed like a whiner.

It wasn't difficult for the 12 of us to agree. She had not made her case. No damages of any kind were levied against the doctors' group.

The doctors celebrated aloud. The woman wept inconsolably.

We came to understand after the trial was over that there had been some drug use by the woman. But neither side brought that up, which really seemed to point to something the doctors did not want to go public. We thought they had made a deal not to bring certain things into evidence. The plaintiff had also presumably lost quite a bit of weight and had become much more attractive. Neither of these facts was available to us for deliberations.

FOUR

COMMUNICATION – I'M WORKIN' IT

Do good work.

~ Garrison Keillor, a line in his standard outcue

MY LIFE IN BUSINESS

Doing good work has always been important to me. I have a killer work ethic. Well, maybe that's a little over the top, since I do know how to relax. But instead of birthing children, I'm way more interested in birthing businesses. First school, then work were places where I found praise and approval. They drove me.

It can be very motivating when even one parent withholds approval, and Dad made that work for me. A parent's message of disapproval sends us on a little spinning wheel of high achievement and excessive striving, like a hamster exercising her little brains out in a never-ending circular chamber. That is, until she resolves the issue and disconnects from the need for parental disapproval.

It was the year 2000 and, professionally, I had gone as far as I could in my small community, or pretty close. The next logical step in my broadcasting career was to move to Los Angeles and get a job, most likely producing news since that's what I knew. I found that once you had a string of one thing on your résumé, it was nearly impossible convincing anyone you could do anything else. And what was on my résumé was a whole bunch of newscasting, news writing, and news production.

I would have loved to produce a documentary or work in entertainment television, but I had never been successful at making my way into the industry in L.A. I had no connections, no family in the business, no money to attend UCLA, and no desire to live there.

I was in love, and that was the other problem. I had fallen in love with San Luis Obispo County on California's Central Coast, and just could not wrench myself away. She had everything: an academic influence, the pristine coastline, culture, clean air, perfect weather, recreation, and a relatively solid economic base, with happy, smart people and a low crime rate.

Jenny McCarthy did a piece on "The Oprah Winfrey Show" where she profiled San Luis Obispo as "the Happiest City in America." I've got to say, I love to travel, but I love to get home just as much. There's no other place like the Central Coast of California. I'm claiming my native-state-of-California status right here.

There are a few disadvantages. SLO has super high housing prices since folks from L.A. and San Francisco are moving in with the gains they got from selling their own upscale homes in those two expensive cities. Homeownership is a pipe dream for most of the SLO population.

Wages are also very low for the most part, with the majority of jobs in the tourist industry. You might be able to find a rental for around $950 if you're lucky, but you'd have been very lucky if you made more than about $1,800 per month in the broadcasting business, and that was on the high side in the mid-1990s. So Jenny McCarthy is right to say plenty of bartering goes on here.

Because wages were low and stagnant, management in small radio stations sometimes let us negotiate trade with restaurants and other businesses. I'm grateful that in my radio days my local dentist traded me some commercial spots for dental work I needed. Randy Voss, DDS, was committed to helping his charity, The Clark Center for the Performing Arts, and in exchange for commercials, he worked on my teeth.

Working in television news at a Santa Maria station, I had become judgmental and disheartened with the personalities and the content of the news I was producing. It was all about ratings:

Stupid sound-bite-sized news, and eye- or ear-catching was the goal. Important stories about what government was doing with tax money just weren't dramatically visual enough to lead the newscast.

I made a conscious and firm declaration to the Universe that I needed work that inspired me, and news was no longer it. At the same time, I was seriously dating a man who looked like my life mate.

So nearly 25 years into the broadcasting business I raised my hands to Heaven. And wouldn't you know it? The Gods heard me when I asked to be finished with the news business.

My career and its path took a dramatic turn when I married Bob and moved to Washington state. I was 45. In the small town where I joined my new husband, there were few news outlets. Sequim had a local newspaper, and neighboring Port Angeles had only one local radio station with one local show on the air. Not much opportunity to work in broadcasting there.

As a side job, I was hired on to the *Sequim Gazette* as a features writer and got to know some of the cool locals. For me, feature writing was more interesting than the harder news.

Bob and I made the decision for me to move to Sequim so he could work the last five years of his job with the school district in order to get his proper retirement pay. And even though I had cried out to my Higher Sources to liberate me from the news business, it was a shock to be in a place where I had let go of my career as well as the closeness of my family and friends through the geographic distance that separated me from these people and paths.

I'd always envisioned being married, but I had come to a place in my life where it would have been all right not to. As a very autonomous Sagittarius, I was true to my sign in marrying later in life. I had dated for 25 years and had a long list of things a mate needed to have if I was going to consider marriage seriously. Bob had everything on the list, which was amazing in itself. Marriage was a dramatic leap into the unknown, but now I had a partner to catch me if I fell too hard, and the safety net he provided allowed me to seriously consider owning my own business.

I experimented with imported goods from Bali, Indonesia: unusual musical instruments, colorfully painted wall mirrors, a wide range of painted wood carvings that included Buddha statues, dragons, drums, and deities. But I was renting booths inside antique stores since I was just experimenting with the product and the market and wanted to keep the overhead low. While I didn't lose a lot of money, I essentially broke even. My intention was to make money while serving others.

So I re-grouped. Bob also had some great ideas and expertise for optimizing an online business but he was still working full time so implementation would take time.

Taking inventory of what I needed from my business life, I resolved one of the top things was to own a business that I could easily relocate to any place we decided we would move to after Bob retired. He was a computer wizard and knew about things like search engine optimization (SEO), HTML language, and programming. So with my hubby/advisor, and my own research into online businesses for dummies, I opened my online store at: www.goddessgift.net

At the same time, I started offering psychic counseling on more than just a part-time basis. Soon it was a big part of my daily life, with several sessions per week.

Only now, people were calling me as an animal communication specialist.

Again, I turned Heavenward.

"Are you sure?" I asked. "I really don't know much about animals."

And the phone would ring with someone asking me for an animal communication consultation.

Years of practice, continuing education on the subject, and top-rate teachers and colleagues spurred me on to develop my abilities. There was a sense of triumph when an animal communication session yielded dramatic results in the harmony of pet-and-people relationships.

And there was heartbreak when I got it wrong. To do good work in this line requires continuing self-examination, practice, clearing, compassion, clear communication, connections with Higher Sources, a grateful heart, and counseling skills, not to mention a healthy dose of confidence that animal communication was real and healing – confidence that was fleeting for a long time in the face of ridicule from doubters,

There are beloved people in my life who don't believe in this skill nor its results. They see animals as less than humans and can't imagine the Divine caring about animals. But they find a way to make it jive with their love for me by giving what I do another title.

My sister says, "Jesus said he would send a comforter," and that's what I am. My other sister says she admires my "relationship with nature." Others respectfully avoid the subject of my telepathic work. And still others discuss it among themselves.

But I am soldiering on, knowing I am doing good work.

TWO PATHS MERGE

Having a whole world of work possibilities open up seems like a great gift, but it can also be daunting. Once I relocated in 2001, I laid out my plans and settled in to figure them out as I incubated the ideas in my new temporary home, waiting for Bob's retirement to open the door to relocating again.

I took stock of my talents and interests.

Top of the list was being able to live anywhere I wanted to since I had no plan to live in Washington state for the long term. With Bob's computer skills, I reasoned that an online retail business was just the ticket and one of the directions I wanted to go to create revenue streams. I also researched the market, found out what sold best online, and began to reconcile this desire with what I wanted to put out into the world.

I'm a spiritual person, a soul in a human form, but the religion of my youth left me feeling abandoned. There were no images of females in the liturgy of the Baptist faith. At least the Catholics had female saints and a couple of Marys, but we didn't. We especially weren't supposed to look at Mary as anything we might want to worship. Emulate, maybe. And there was wa-a-ay too much Hell, damnation and threat in the Baptist doctrine for me.

I sought the God of Love and I wanted comfort and inspiration from my Higher Sources, and while I was at it, I wanted some female images to relate to as well.

As a believer in honoring all paths to the Divine, I decided on a business that put a female face on God, honoring the feminine side of divinity. I opened **www.goddessgift.net** with a dozen small statues of multi-cultural Goddesses. I put it on a credit card, and when I sold one small statue I bought two.

At the same time, I continued to read and study telepathic communication with animals and soon created a website for that work as well at **www.telepathictalk.com**. Counseling was a gift I was meant for, a natural path I could share that would serve both me and my fellow travelers.

Both businesses have brought me great joy and great challenges. The path toward full self-acceptance of my views, ideas, and gifts seems long and is always unfolding. It was challenging when my dad thought that I was out to defraud the public with my telepathic abilities, or that my Goddess business was about man-hating.

These perspectives were so far afield of who I am: a person of high integrity intent on service. But OWN came to my rescue with a Life Class that Oprah did with Dr. Brene Brown. She introduced me to the idea that you can be either comfortable or courageous, but not both. Another Life Class helping me on my journey.

So I'm willing to risk and I'm willing to play big. I've stepped out of the norm. Making history, being on the cutting edge of rediscovering our sixth-sense talents is not a place of comfort much of the time. You can feel people's disapproval and you can often hear it as well. I'm afraid and brave at the same time.

I'm comforted by Dr. Brown's quote from Theodore Roosevelt:

> It is not the critic who counts; not the man who points out how the strong man stumbles, or where the doer of deeds could have done them better. The credit belongs to the man who is actually in the arena, whose face is marred by dust and sweat and blood; who strives valiantly, who in the end may know the triumph of high achievement but when he fails, he does so daring greatly.

Dr. Brown decided, "That's who I want to be. If we want to be courageous and we want to be in the arena, we're gonna get our butts kicked. There is no other option."

[And] when the "Twitter Thugs" came calling on her, she said, "If you are also not in the arena getting your butt kicked, I'm not interested in your feedback."

Yeah. Me too. And I still work on it.

LANGUAGES OF LOVE AND LAUGHTER

In my nuclear family, we were always frank and brutally direct, and I was pretty much allowed to express my true feelings. That led the way to acceptance of some non-traditional communication methods, some of which we created as a family of women.

We were inventors of languages. As kids, we all used pig Latin with one another and that language evolved into others. We also have spoken Deep South, black ghetto, surfer, Valley girl, some Spanish, some Arabic, "Madea," and our own private languages.

I loved foreign languages and Mom was always interested in learning too, so she repeated and mastered words and phrases in Spanish and in Arabic, the languages I studied in school.

We are all proficient at speaking in accents from Alabama and Georgia too. Once, a woman from the Deep South who was sensitive to "Southern bashing" came to visit Mom's house. When she and I broke out into our extreme Southern drawl, the guest's defenses reared up. She was wise enough to inquire further as to our accents, though, so I explained.

"We have many people we love in the Deep South. Many of our most beloved family members hail from Georgia and Alabama, so I guess it gives us the right."

We watched one of my favorite movies that day with our visiting friends in which some classic Texas accents were prominent in the characterizations. The movie is called "Bernie," and it stars Jack Black, Shirley MacLaine, and Matthew McConaughey. But the very best line in the movie belongs to a more minor character, a middle-aged blonde, when she says, "Honey, anybody around here would a give fah dollahs to shoot that woman dayown."

The language we invented that is unique to us is not easily understood by others. We replace all letter "l's" with "n's." "Lucky lady" becomes "nucky nady" and so on. This language is always used in fun with my hilarious mama, who's always open to playing with words and accents. We also have dozens of nicknames for one another.

These languages have given the men in our lives a run for their money. Most of the time brothers and sons-in-law don't have any idea what the "hail" we are saying. Now and then we try and teach them, usually for naught. Which works out fine, actually.

Like many folks, we have also dealt with other languages as we grew up, including the languages of criticism, anger, and jealousy.

When I married Bob, he brought compassion and some modesty into the family. He stated that in our household there would be no more name-calling. I was in total agreement and asked Mom to participate. I did this by declaring "no name-calling" when she did it, which was pretty often. We kept it light, but she agreed to go along with the new rule – or at least try to.

Every now and then she got a little frustrated. She would say things like, "That bumble-headed, nitwit store clerk made me so mad –" then . . . she'd stop and look confused. "Oh wait," she'd ask, "was that name-calling?"

Usually, we would dissolve into laughter. But she got much better at the no-name-calling rule because she really agreed with it.

FIVE

I TALK WITH ANIMALS

Some people talk to animals. Not many listen though.
That's the problem.

~ A. A. Milne, *Winnie the Pooh*

HEALING IN THE CANYON:
LITTLE MAN, THE MINIATURE HORSE

In the quiet light of the stable, you hear a muffled snort, a stamp of a hoof, a friendly nicker. Gentle eyes inquire, "How are you, old friend?" and suddenly, all your troubles fade away

~ Author Unknown

Here I was, a mental health advocate and counseling care professional, and I had to take notice of how very difficult it was for me to make an appointment with a counselor. Even though I thought counseling was incredibly important and necessary for good mental health, and even though I recommended it to many people, it was surprisingly hard for me to come to the decision to make an appointment with a professional.

I was working on marriage and business issues, specifically how to regain my autonomy after my husband's retirement. There were tears of sadness in the session with Daphne related to problems I couldn't seem to fix in the relationship. She had me take a written test called the Beck's Inventory, a 21-question inventory that quantifies how depressed a person is or isn't.

"Really?" I asked in surprise as she reported the results.

"Yes, you are moderately depressed," she said, recommending that I get my hormone levels checked just in case it was physical.

The next afternoon, thoughts of my miniature horse companion were prominent. So I followed the intuitive message to the canyon to seek solace in nurturing him with treats and grooming his body. I took him ears of corn, oatmeal, and bananas, some of his favorites.

He didn't seem to feel very well. He ate less and his nose and bad eye were runny. His belly was filled with gas and bloated.

The guinea hens, his constant companions, were very nervous. They followed us everywhere and stayed right at Little Man's heels, squawking at me. They were so close, in fact, that he stumbled into them a few times while we took a walk through the grass of a peaceful garden, and then along the dirt road.

The hens' unusually loud and frantic behavior alerted me to their concern for Little Man's health and safety. They had never followed us before, but they stayed in step, squawking more loudly when the little horse stumbled while navigating through some tangled garden hoses across the road.

I asked the animals if they could help me heal myself and Little Man was the first to say yes. We already had an agreement that he would be one of my animal counselors after he left his body, and he acted as a calming influence when I visited him in the canyon too.

After our short walk around, I produced the day's treats for him, then stood with my arm around his neck. He turned his head around often, on the side of his one good eye, to softly nuzzle my pants leg.

Poor little old man. He was 32 and his little feet could hardly carry his swollen body. Many people who loved him stopped by with a variety of foodstuffs, and most recently Miss Judy, a former hot walker from Kentucky, had taken over his care. I was thankful, because even though Little Man and I kept in touch daily telepathically, it was a half-hour ride with a substantial gasoline bill every time I drove to visit him.

Miss Judy lived very close to Little Man, and she knew things about horses I didn't know.

As Little Man and I stood there that day, tears ran down my cheeks, but when I left the canyon I felt recovered, stronger, determined, and had a few ideas for resolving some of the things that were troubling me.

It was autumn. I planned to spend Saturday looking for a horse blanket for Little Man to spend the winter in, although I wondered if he would last through the cold days in the canyon. There was a plan afoot to reinforce his structure and I was on board to help build it.

Little Man's presence never failed to help heal me. After being with him I was always renewed somehow, blessed with clearer vision. Grateful for his gifts, I left him peacefully grazing and headed home.

LITTLE MAN MOVES ON

It was mid-summer 2012, two full years later, when I got word from Judy that Little Man's people were making plans to put him down. He was very unsteady on his feet, had fallen down twice, and had been unable to get himself up. No one wanted him to suffer.

He was getting skinny. He was having a hard time digesting his food and his eyesight was worsening. When I arrived at his enclosure I was distracted by grief and the thought of him not being there someday soon. I wanted to talk with him about impending events and how he felt about euthanasia.

After many years of doing the animal communication work, it still sounded pretty nutty when I said an animal had told me something, but I came to the realization that it was all semantics. It is more accurate to say that animals send us a feeling of this or that, and we translate that feeling into words. So when I went to see the miniature pony I had come to love and appreciate so much, the feelings washed over me, carried by a warm summer wind.

He opened the conversation, sending me a message. "This is the most beautiful, glorious day – let's enjoy it. This is a wonderful place."

Here was my teacher once again. My difficult emotions were immediately soothed. He was focused in the moment, feeling the breeze and the sun on his back. I went into action grooming him gently. The insects were beginning to gather on his hair, attracted by the pungent smell of him. He was still shedding a cold weather undercoat and there were several piles of snow-white hair when I was through. We spent an hour in gratitude for one another, just being. Like most animals, he was a master of that.

I noticed he allowed me to touch him even in the places he had resisted before. His sensitive sinuses had been off limits, and the skin of his head was thin because there was no fat to protect it. Brushing under his chin where his little skull was practically inverted was out of the question, but he enjoyed it when I groomed his neck. I offered some TTouch™ healing as well, which he accepted (Linda Tellington-Jones' revolutionary Tellington bodywork method).

Little Man was as active as I'd seen him for several months. He walked around smelling the different grasses in his fenced yard. He switched his tail at flies and snorted. I knew it was the death walk. I reflected on how it might be when he passed, he showed me he would fly free of his body.

"Like Pegasus?" I asked him.

"Yes, just like that," he showed me in a vision.

"We'll stay in touch when you've left the body behind though, right?" I asked for reassurance.

"Of course," he said, "I will always be there to help."

He asked me to send gratitude and love to all those who had taken such good care of him, and he showed me that there had been talk of putting him down years before. Instead, half a dozen people came together to make this little grassy enclosure work for him. They'd built a shelter in the sunshine just for him, where he had enjoyed many different kinds of animal friends. He shared his grain with birds, chickens, and guinea hens. He had learned to live next to the road, where people drove by slowly to say hello to him. We had worked together on the trauma of four-wheeler and loud motorcycle-type vehicles that startled him in the normally quiet canyon. He felt much safer after those talks.

What always struck me with Little Man is how he was able to transform any difficult emotional mood I was undergoing. Today was no different. As I came, full of grief, into his yard, I was caught off guard when his first thoughts toward me were about what a beautiful summer day he was enjoying. Here I was mired in the sorrow of a future event, and Little Man was firmly planted in the moment.

He let me know that he wouldn't be around for much longer, and that whatever his people had to do was all right. He felt that their decision to euthanize him came from a loving intent.

His primary human companion, Samantha, arrived soon after my love fest with Little Man began. She brought him a banquet of his favorite foods: cantaloupe, corn tortillas, bananas, corn on the cob, and apple pie. He was full from breakfast and couldn't eat them, but he did enjoy the smells just as well and he appreciated the love that came with the foods. Later, he enjoyed the other creatures in the canyon who came to share some of these treats, and he was also able to get some of the food down.

"How did you find out he liked these particular foods?" Judy asked Samantha.

"When Little Man wandered around freely all over our land, we used to barbeque outside," Samantha said. "We'd put tortillas on the grill and he would steal them. We'd be looking all over wondering where the corn tortillas were and finally we caught him!"

When I left the canyon I was full of gratitude not only for Little Man and his gifts, but for Samantha too. She had spent her time and money for several years enabling me to have at least part of the care and love of a wonderful miniature pony. My gratitude extended to Miss Judy too, who had watched over him every day with loving care. As I looked in the enclosure where his food was kept, there was no grain soaking in water for the next day's feed. His lack of appetite made this daily ritual no longer necessary.

Little Man told me he was not sure the plan for euthanasia that his people had would come together before he passed. The men in charge of lining up the vet and excavating the gravesite were busy with other big projects. I told him it would be easiest on the people if he were to pass in the night and he took the information in. Still, I felt as if he had some purpose in allowing the human plan to go through. We would have to wait and see how it all played out, but I was sure it would be less than a month before Little Man would be moving on.

I wanted to be in attendance if I was allowed, but I also knew some of the players in the euthanasia event thought I was a little crazy. I could also feel worry. Often people are concerned about messages from their animal friends that might be offered at inopportune times. Not realizing how truly sensitive many animals are, people are sometimes afraid you're going to tell them painful things or try and interfere with their plans.

I wanted to send Little Man on his way in celebration, and to feel the release from the body when his soul flew free. The jury was out on whether or not Little Man's people would let me experience those precious moments. I crossed my fingers that they would allow me to send my friend off on his journey.

In the end I was informed that Little Man's people had chosen a date to euthanize him. The appointment with the vet would be at 11 a.m. on a Thursday in June. I made my way to the canyon an hour earlier.

It was a gorgeous day when I arrived at Little Man's enclosure, and several canyon residents who had loved him over the years were in attendance. A few of his close human companions could not be there because they were too emotional.

Little Man was optimistic about his impending journey. He commented again on the beauty of the day and said it was a good day to make the transition. He said he knew these people were gathered for him and that he felt love all around. He also commented that he knew he was the guest of honor at the party.

The miniature pony was adorned with his bridle so he could be more easily led to the grassy hill where he would spend his last hours. His human dad, John, was in attendance to reassure the pony who had been a part of his family for so many years.

Little Man was more active than he had been in many, many months. There were half a dozen people there to send him on his way and each of us in turn stood between the little horse and any equipment, tree, or object he might run into as he walked around.

Pretty close to being blind in both eyes by then, he explored different things by bumping into them, often bruising his bad eye. He walked all around the Los Berros Canyon Peace Park just across the street from his enclosure while we all nervously awaited the tardy veterinarian, who had to attend to an unexpected emergency.

The gravesite would be in a shady area, and it was a beautiful, peaceful place. Little Man approved of the site.

Some of the folks there to witness the event were concerned that he was so active.

"Is he nervous or anxious?" the grieving Judy asked me.

"No. He's generating energy to separate the soul from the body," I told her.

Several of us laid healing hands on Little Man as the vet gave him the tranquilizer that would calm him for the final injection. As the vet reached to find the vein in his neck, we stabilized the wavering pony, forming a human chain around him to hold him up.

"Go ahead and just let him lie down," the vet told us.

Little Man's knees went weak and we laid him down on his side tenderly. Human hands on his body transmitted love as we quietly murmured, "Go in love, Little Man" and "Go in peace, my pony boy." The vet gave him the final injection. Little Man took three deep breaths and was gone.

The men there carefully pulled his body into the giant hole in the ground, gently placing him with his little head in the shade. I threw yellow daisies in after him, then he was covered with a lightweight blanket. The tractor filled in the hole.

Later that day I brought a lovely framed picture of him and set it on the fence near the gravesite, then placed a colorful Hawaiian lei around the portrait.

The little horse who had served so many children at the county fair as their first horse experience was gone. The little horse who had soothed my own tears was now in spirit. I sent him love for the journey and a request for him to stay in touch.

INSPIRATION FROM BIG HEAD, THE FERAL CAT

Big Head was one of those cases of inspirational proof to me that I was firmly in the flow of things and that the Holy Spirit and I were in cahoots regarding my mission of healing animals and their people.

An urgent call from Christy, a client, alerted me to an injured feral orange tabby cat with huge yellow eyes and an extra-large head who was living near Santa Cruz, Calif.

Christy said she had been feeding him and that it looked as if someone in the neighborhood had cut him, leaving him bloody all around his back end.

Because he was feral, Big Head didn't come too close to humans, but Christy wanted to help him out, and she wanted me to see if he would allow her to capture him.

I found him easy to contact. He said he had a great affection for this kindhearted woman of good intent. Nonetheless, he sent me a feeling that he would not be seen for a few days. I asked him to let me take a look at his wounds via remote viewing, and got confirmation that the bleeding had stopped. From her sightings, Christy agreed that the blood she saw looked dry, so the matter was a little bit less urgent than it had been a day earlier.

Of course, as all animals do, Big wanted all the details about what was going to happen. I showed him the cat carrier, the van that would take him to the vet, and how the humans would likely help him once he arrived at the clinic.

I also let him know that this was how we took care of him, and that we were interested in him having a different kind of experience with humans than the violence he had suffered.

Finally, I pulled out the big guns, adding that he could advance animal communication if he decided to cooperate.

I didn't hold out much hope for an injured feral cat to agree to what I showed Big.

But Big Head surprised me! He told me he was willing to allow Christy to help him out. I had to double check what I was hearing. I then told Christy to look for him at her back door in a couple of days' time.

Two days later, the big orange cat showed up at Christy's kitchen door and offered himself up for the vet visit. He easily allowed her to pick him up and put him in the carrier.

The veterinarian said it was one of the worst cases she had ever seen of animal abuse. He'd lost a lot of blood and a lot of necrotic tissue had to be removed. It appeared as if he'd been held in a towel or bag as someone sliced his testicles with razor blades.

Big Head came through the vet visit with flying colors. I followed closely for the next week, sending him gratitude for allowing us to intervene and checking on his healing progress.

The last time I contacted him, he was enjoying solitude as he recovered in a bathroom, relaxing in a cozy bed and thinking about making a big change to a mostly inside life instead of the life he'd led outside.

Christy was willing to have a chat with her other cats about Big Head moving in. After feeding Big outside for a long time, Christy was delighted to welcome him into her home.

As an aside, I asked Big Head about his name and if he'd prefer another since I thought this one a little impersonal. He made me laugh when he said it brought all kinds of images to mind for humans and that it was mostly humorous to them.

He said he'd keep it!

MY WET PET

My beloved chow chow, Rusti, had been a spirit dog for a year when thoughts of hooking up with a new animal friend crossed my mind. But a deal I'd made five years earlier caught up with me, making animal companionship an illusive notion. And anyway, the Divine Unseen had other plans for my next rather unconventional animal companion.

Before we were married, my husband asked me if I would consider living without my dog and two cats. It was practically our first date and I said I would consider it if we got serious, but I insisted that it definitely would not happen until Rusti and my two cats, Bosley and Batgirl, had passed on.

After we were married, Bob was wonderful with the animals, caring for them tenderly and loving them deeply. But he keenly felt that the responsibility for animals and the inevitable loss when they died was too hard for him to take. Severe allergies, along with a resistance to taking medication, added to his perspective.

Seven years later, all my animals were spirit helpers from the other side, and in all fairness, it was my husband's turn to have his way and live without the daily care and consideration that animal companions require.

A move three states away meant that our new living situation didn't support having animals either. It was far less than ideal for a cat or a dog to join us in our tiny new living space.

"So what would be the perfect animal companion in my current situation?" I asked my Higher Source. The answer was right in front of me, or more precisely, on the north side of the house.

This is the side of our home adjacent to a culvert that carries rainwater and other runoff to the ocean. Teeming with life, it's filled with all manner of creatures that come and go seasonally, including dragonflies and a variety of other insects, ducks, and little frogs.

We had a problem with the door on that north side: A half-inch gap underneath it allowed spring breezes to waft in, and it wasn't long before something else squeezed in under the door: tiny frog visitors.

At first they seemed to come in small families of four. A couple of them would hop on in, sometimes loitering behind the bookcase for a while, sometimes climbing the wall with their little sucker feet. One of them would scale the wall half way up, jump into the cut-out eyes on a wooden giraffe mask that hung there, and hibernate behind the wood. Eventually, they all ended up in the water-filled vase with the lucky bamboo plants, where they could lounge on a stalk half in and half out of the water.

For several weeks each night around dinnertime, a mama frog would slip in underneath the door and wait just inside. After a few minutes, a couple of juvenile frogs inevitably appeared from inside the house, and followed her out.

I welcomed them all in, marveling at their chameleon skin and watching it change colors right in front of my eyes whenever they moved from clinging to a bamboo stalk to the light wooden table the bamboo arrangement sat on. As an inter-species communicator, I naturally opened the lines of discussion immediately.

Our initial communication was about what parts of the house would be safest for them. I let them know that humans are not always cognizant of their feet, which can injure tiny amphibians. Their listening skills were impeccable, and rarely did they make a mistake and venture outside the area I asked them to stay in. Once in a while, when they did, we herded them gently back to their safe zone.

Our second conversation revolved around relieving themselves outside.

After a month or so, I began to recognize their energy, and one of them in particular visited daily. I called him Frogger and delighted in his company.

"This is what human love and respect feels like," I told him, sending those sentiments his way.

He took it in. He came back for more on subsequent days and told his friends.

"I really would like to touch you," I said to my frog friend one day, as he floated in the plant water. "Humans love to touch. Will you let me?" I asked. He didn't really want me to, but my enthusiasm trampled down my desire to respect his space.

Frogger jumped a little to the side of the bowl as my finger came gently into contact with his back, saying his instinct was to hop away, but he stayed and I apologized for not being able to resist touching him.

I also shared worry with him.

"I'm concerned there's nothing for you to eat here," I told him.

"There's plenty for me to eat here," he said, "you just can't see it."

I admired Frogger's efficiency when it came to swimming, a sport I also enjoyed. He treaded water without having to wave his arms around like me. He just naturally floated.

Settling in further in our new location meant repairs, and as the weather got cooler, Bob and I installed weather stripping at the bottom of the door to keep the cold out. I was greatly saddened that Frogger would no longer be able to visit spontaneously and it weighed heavily on my mind for a few days. Then one morning I got up and looked in the lucky bamboo only to find his little head poking above the water!

"Frogger!" I said. "I'm so happy you found a way in!"

But had he? I was concerned. What if he had been hiding in the house for a couple of days and couldn't get out? I had to know, so as soon as he began hopping along the wall toward the door jamb, his normal exit strategy, I asked him.

"Please show me if you need my help getting out of the house and back to your frog family," I said.

Frogger was slow. He hopped. He stopped. He changed direction a few times and hopped around, but didn't go out.

"I guess you'll need a little help then," I said, and with that, I opened the door. He could easily feel the cool night air, smell the fog, and hear the sounds of his fellow frogs in the culvert outside. Yet he hopped away from the door once it was open and waited patiently nearby.

I closed the door and sat back, waiting to hear what he was trying to convey. After a few minutes, he proceeded to a tiny separation between the weather stripping and the door jamb, flattened his body, and wiggled his way out through the small crack. It was an amazing magical feat in which he reduced his body size by half! It took a great deal of effort and I congratulated him, thanking him for showing me his escape route and setting my mind at ease.

Frogger was so clever and our communication was going so well, my joy at having him as a companion increased until one day I offered him a proposition.

"How would you like to be a star and contribute to inter-species harmony?" I asked him. "I'm going to write up our story and I need some photos. What that means is that there will be a flash of light and I'll be getting pretty close to you. But you'll be safe. I'm only admiring your good looks"

I thought I heard Frogger agree to pose, but I wasn't sure. (It's harder to be objective once you're emotionally involved!)

The photo op would prove challenging when the new camera I used was difficult to focus correctly. I informed my wet companion of my dilemma, told him that it might take more than one try, and asked for his patience.

He sat quite still for a full set of more than a dozen flashing photos. I plugged the camera into the computer and waited. All blurry. Drat.

When I returned from viewing the photos on the computer in another room, he hadn't moved a muscle. "Sorry, Frogger. But I failed this round. I need to try again," I told him as I geared up for another round of photos.

Another dozen more flashing photographs were also problematic.

"Sorry, again," I said, returning from viewing the second set of pictures. He still hadn't moved as I proceeded to shoot a third round of photos.

Three times was the charm as the pictures materialized on the computer screen. I laughed and laughed at seeing Frogger's face up close. He had Andy Rooney eyebrows, a wide smile, and looked like a Chinese scholar. My respect for his ancient species humbled me, but my smile was ear to ear as I looked at his close-ups.

Approaching the bowl where he was floating in the water, I told him I had gotten the photos and thanked him for his patience. I told him what fun it was to see his wise face. At that, he immediately dove down into the water in the bamboo bowl with a plop! He had agreed to allow me to get the photos I wanted, no matter how long it took me, but once it was done, he was gone.

After that we made agreements that worked about 90 percent of the time. Our rules included: One or two adult frogs in the house at a time, do your business outside, stay in the living room along the wooden flooring, come over anytime, and bring the kids if you want.

I was full of gratitude for my new friends and their seasonal nightly chorus, which rose like a wave of a million chirping voices, then crashed into silence all at once. Frog lullabies rocked me to sleep, and I enjoyed perfect animal companionship with Frogger, his friends, and his family.

WHEN YOU LOSE A BELOVED ANIMAL COMPANION

The agony of losing a beloved animal friend is brought home to me on a weekly basis as an animal communicator. My heart goes out to those who are either missing an animal companion that has passed or have lost one. In the midst of their heartache, these clients want to know if their animal is going through the same kind of pain that they are experiencing.

Well, not exactly.

WHEN YOUR PET DIES

Animals live in the present moment, and it's one of the things we love most about them. When we've been angry with them, scolded them, or even mistreated them, they hold no grudge. Unless the abuse is long term and unrelenting, dogs offer a tentative approach as they keep coming back, although cats will often strike out on their own.

"I miss Buster so much, I can hardly function," Betsy told me during her session. She had hired me to get in touch with her sweet boxer, who had left his body just a few weeks before. "Does he miss me as much as I miss him?" she wanted to know.

This is where the counseling and diplomacy part of my skill as an animal communicator comes in, because Buster does not miss her in the way she's thinking. Remember, animals always live in the now.

"Buster does not exactly feel the separation the way you do," I explain. "He simply left an ailing body that no longer served him, and now he is right at your side again as a spirit dog. He feels your grief and is staying very close. In fact, he says you have felt him on the bed next to you when you sleep."

"That's funny! I have actually felt a weight on the bed exactly where he would have been, but when I wake up nothing is there," she reports. It's Buster, all right, I tell her.

WHEN YOU LOSE A PET

Lost pets offer a different kind of challenge. Frightened by an unfriendly dog, cat, truck, or other kind of trauma, they can just take off running and lose their bearings, especially if the weather changes.

Some have just gone for a romp, and a good old adventure turns into a situation where they've approached a kind person, gotten into a car, and found themselves in a different home. Their life purposes, like ours, are meant to evolve, and, like us, they do that through a variety of experiences.

"My cat, Neo, is missing," says a frantic caller. She deeply loves her pet, but her husband doesn't. When I tune in to Neo he sends me the feeling that his life is threatened.

"My human dad imagines running over cats as a game with points," Neo tells me sadly.

I don't relay the information quite like that.

"Neo says there is someone in the household who doesn't like cats," I tell my client, who confesses that her husband tolerates Neo, but would rather not live with a cat. Meanwhile, Neo has found a single lady who enjoys his company and is feeding him on her back porch. She's considering letting him inside when I connect with him telepathically.

Does that mean he no longer loves his original human mom? No.

Love transcends all of these boundaries. But it does mean that Neo is likely to make a change in his living situation. He will give up creature comforts of living indoors for a wilder existence where he hunts, curls up in a drafty barn inside his warm fur coat, and where the new woman will care for him by providing food and water and a few kind words on a daily basis. To Neo, it doesn't feel as if he's given up or abandoned his first human family. It's just that the circumstances have changed.

A significant number of animal communicators do not offer lost animal help, partly due to the overwhelming emotions clients bring to the session. Also, messages sent by the animal can be ambiguous. Using remote viewing techniques, I can see what the animal sees, but since pets don't read street signs, the clues can be anything from a house with purple trim to five miles down the road in an easterly direction.

Messages can also be crystal clear. Recently I told a family that a man would bring their dog to the shelter and they would be reunited there. All they had to do was wait a few days. That's just what happened, but the waiting was agonizing.

People who love their lost animals often look for someone to blame for their despair. In their grief, they are unable to see another point of view. That was the case with Teddy the missing tabby's human mom.

"I see Teddy living in a house with a woman and one other cat. He's being well cared for, says he has good food, and the blonde woman is very kind to him," I told her.

"Hasn't she seen the posters? Why hasn't she called the local shelters? Doesn't she know Teddy is my cat?" Johnna said through angry tears.

"The woman found Teddy hungry and sick and even though he had a collar on, her point of view was that she was saving his life, not stealing him from a loving human companion," I said.

This can be upsetting news in itself because if animals are being well treated, they see little reason to depart from their new home, especially if they've left a high-stress or partially hostile environment.

"Doesn't he know I'm devastated?" Johnna asked. And there's that problem again. Teddy picks up on his human's distress, but devastation is an emotion that projects both into the future and into the past, so in some ways it is out of the realm of experience for "living-in-the-moment" animals.

To complicate matters further, it's just that kind of high-level emotional distress that will wave a red flag of anxiety, keeping an animal from coming back. Negative emotions can sometimes be like a beacon of animal repellent, another reason why some animal communicators don't work on these cases. The human piece of the puzzle has to be resolved first.

Waiting and wondering can be torture, but sometimes knowing that your pet is being well cared for by a new family is just as distressing. Seeking someone to blame is a trap under those circumstances. Focus instead on the needs of your precious pet. Honor his evolutionary blueprint, which could include a variety of living situations and experiences – advice that's certainly easier said than done.

We are not in control of our priceless animal companions. We are simply lucky enough to intertwine our lives with theirs for a time. How long that time is has already been determined.

SIX

LESS-TRAVELED PATHS TO HEALING

For me, singing sad songs often has a way of healing a situation. It gets the hurt out in the open into the light, out of the darkness.

~ Reba McEntire

PAST LIFE REGRESSION

> While it might be entertaining to fantasize about famous past lives, it is just a distraction. The real point is to see and understand the karmic patterns of our lives, and their roots in an endless repetitive cycle that traps us in unconscious behavior.
> ~ Osho Zen Tarot

Whether you believe you have lived before, whether you can conceive of parallel alternate dimensions or realities that are non-physical, or whether that kind of talk seems like fantasy, successful outcomes from past life regression in my practice are hardly arguable.

In my own life and in the lives of clients I've served through past life regressions, our ability to go to places and events that still live within our imaginations and cellular memories to make us whole again is astounding. Regression has gently unlocked me from compulsive, irrational attachments in my own life, as well as healing wounds that defy medical diagnosis and treatment in the lives of my clients.

MY SESSION WITH SARAH

One of the first times I turned to past life regression to help me with an unnatural attachment, I was liberated from it forever. My friend Sarah, a past life regression therapist, helped me with an unexplained and intense longing that might have led me into becoming a deranged, celebrity- stalking fan.

Relaxing deeply as I followed Sarah's suggestion, I allowed images to flow into my mind.

I was swimming in a sea of dead bodies, the dark blue ocean around me filled with the smell of gunpowder. Terrified, but feeling lucky to be alive, I witnessed the fin of a shark careening by in the too-near distance, as the fish dragged body parts below the surface in silent determination. With the blood of my fellow sailors floating on the water, big fish were taking advantage of easy pickings.

Dazed but aware that I had been blown from my ship by the mighty blast of an enemy cannon, I could see the huge vessel that had been my home for many months about 100 feet behind me. From a perspective above the scene I viewed myself dressed in what looked like a British Royal Navy uniform from the 1800s. My thoughts screamed survival and I turned quickly to my brother, my unfortunate companion in this God-forsaken watery death trap.

Gaining my bearings, I spotted him about 10 feet away. I was blinded by a singular purpose – nothing mattered more than swimming to save him from the sharks and the heavy artillery. As he floated face down in the water, I reached him quickly, turned him over, and cradled him in a headlock. Paddling with all the strength of my one free arm and my legs, I pulled him to shore as quickly as I could swim.

Frantically, I tried to revive him. Mouth to mouth, pumping his chest wildly to free the water from his lungs, crying to the heavens, then back to breathing into him – this was my cycle, but my efforts came too late. My beloved brother, my light in the darkness of military service, was gone. Tears and agony followed as I lay my head on his chest, sobbing. The longing for him lasted longer than that one lifetime.

As I found my way back to the present reality, my eyes filled with tears. I had come to see my friend Sarah to find out why I felt so attached to the actress and author, Shirley MacLaine. I knew myself as a reasonable human being, but I had a totally irrational longing to know her. I missed her mightily, yet I had never met her. I felt personally proud when she made an appearance, starred in a new movie, or wrote a new book. How could that be? It just didn't make any rational sense.

The visions helped explain these strange emotions for me, and the session liberated me from the intensity of missing her, and from becoming some kind of stalker, intent on embracing Shirley in a flood of joyful tears of reunion. The trauma was unlocked and the hold on me that had existed before was gone.

My session with Sarah that day revealed that Shirley MacLaine and I were brothers in that lifetime. Now that we're women and strangers, my love for her still runs deep, but it's no longer inexplicable. More than a fan, I hope one day to meet her in this physical world, so that I might give her that hug reserved for my long-lost brother.

She's one of the people in the world who wouldn't think I'd lost my mind entirely if I shared this story with her, although I'm sure she gets many such inquiries. She understands that there are great mysteries of the unseen universe unfolding every day, and that my story is entirely possible. She's also likely to agree with me that what some people call coincidence is what I call synchronicity: those times when our Higher Selves put us directly in the path of what we need to see or know.

'THE TODAY SHOW'

Four years following this regression, on an October day in the middle of the work week, a chill in the air and impending rain made me feel like cuddling up under a blanket. Turns out the urge to stay home was purposeful because although the time to begin my work day was upon me, I lazily postponed my morning exercise ritual, hoping the weather would clear. Feeling a little guilty, I turned on the television, and tuned in to "The Today Show."

"Even from birth, she was destined to be a star," said co-host Matt Laurer. "Named after Shirley Temple, she saw her name in light for the first time in 1955 along side John Forsythe in 'The Trouble with Harry.' "

While a few of Shirley MacLaine's early film clips appeared on the screen, Laurer went on to read a short bio that included her Oscar for Best Actress in 1983 for "Terms of Endearment." Then he touted her work as a prolific author. Because her 10th book, *Out On A Leash*, had just been released, she had temporarily left her ranch in New Mexico, trekking to Manhattan to talk about it. Laurer explained that the book was "an exploration of reality and love."

Excited and grateful that Spirit had guided me to the early morning television program, my guilt dissolved into childish delight. Seeing her on the small screen provided joy, inspiration, and, of course, an immediate desire to buy her book.

Shirley's life and perspective and mine have parallels. We're both animal lovers and have both experienced the contentment and the multi-dimensional relationship one can have with a dog. We've both been public figures. I spent a dozen years in the broadcasting business, becoming a radio and television personality in my California community, and that's a path that requires examination of how one feels about public approval. Shirley and I have the same perspective when it comes to that, although she's a lot more advanced than I am, no longer needing approval from an outside source. During the interview, she provided an admirable example of where I'm aiming.

Laurer explained that in *Out On A Leash*, Shirley writes one chapter, then her dog, Terry, writes the next.

"What do you say to the viewer, Shirley, who says, 'But she's saying that the dog writes every other chapter' and has a difficult time taking that seriously?" Laurer asked.

Shirley laughed.

"Oh, that is really *their* problem," she said, smiling. "I'm so sorry for them."

She went on to explain that what really happens when people read her book is that they're left wondering what *their* dog thinks of *them*. Often with readers, she said, a reversal of perspectives and a consciousness-raising related to animals occurs.

Laurer continued probing.

"Are you at a stage in life where you simply don't care what other people think?" he asked her after the commercial break.

"Oh, sure," she said matter-of-factly. "Why should I care? It's none of my business."

"Go, girl!" I said to the TV, as I thoughtfully considered the path she must have taken to reach that level of self-acceptance.

Shirley's prickly path through Hollywood – what she calls "the big knife" – would have taken her to self-acceptance or made her crazy, depending.

The recipe for success in Hollywood includes intense scrutiny from casting agents, producers, directors, and others, all focused on how you look, walk, feel, act, and talk. Combine those ingredients with more rejection than the normal person experiences in a lifetime, fold that in with the human vulnerability of youth, middle age, or advanced years, and a person has to either get tough or get drugs in order to alleviate the pain of the daily beating. From this brutal professional path, she has risen.

Shirley and I also share a communication style. On "The Today Show" she helped me understand why. I spent years honing my communication skills, looking for the part of me that is the compassionate communicator, searching for my diplomatic self.

Accused of being too brutally honest, I've found my voice now, the one that nurtures, while expressing nothing less than my truth. Shirley got this lesson and this gift from her terrier, Terry, she said.

"I couldn't be a person who would confuse others by not saying what I really feel," she tells us from the TV screen, as Terry looks intently in her direction from a sheepskin mat on the studio floor.

"So what I get from Terry is this feminine point of view. She never denies what she really feels."

I couldn't be a person who would confuse others either, my friend. Thank you for clarifying that for me.

Laurer remarks that dog is God spelled backwards. To me, caring for one is a sacred trust and an unequalled gift of pure, unconditional love. There is no judgment on the part of a dog: no observational ridicule. A dog trusts completely, with no shame and no pride, until his trust is broken. In that is an intimacy not easily found with people.

When "The Today Show" went to commercial again and on to another subject, I was renewed. The voyeuristic pleasure of seeing her resulted in my sending a little prayer of gratitude to the producers, and to my brother, Shirl.

DONNA'S LABORED BREATHING

Past life regression helped me, and it also helped Donna, who came to see me in hopes of gaining a better understanding of a nagging health concern that made no logical sense to her. A woman in her 60s, Donna had spells where she felt she couldn't breathe, even though she was fit and exercised daily.

Like many clients, Donna felt she couldn't be regressed. She'd had trouble with visualizing in the past, and she didn't think she was capable of "going under" in a relaxed state of heightened awareness. But three lifetimes came through that seemed directly related to her breathing problems.

In the first, she was a little girl who had died at an early age from tuberculosis. Only six or seven years old at the time of her death, she felt her breathing being choked off. Typical symptoms of TB include a cough that is often worse in the morning, chest pain, breathlessness, night sweats, and signs of pneumonia. A doctor's exam with a stethoscope may reveal diminished breath sounds, bronchial breathing, tracheal deviation, and coarse crackles. I didn't know this at the time of the reading, but found out after the session that TB was indeed a lung ailment.

Clearing the remnants of the disease that were left over in the cellular memory of her present body, we moved on to the next relevant death Donna experienced.

In her second lifetime, Donna had been a sickly man in his 30s, suffering from pneumonia or lung problems. On his deathbed, surrounded by his wife and children, he lay racked with guilt about leaving his family at such a young age with no way to earn a living. He knew his family's life would be hard, and Donna had internalized some of the guilt from his early departure. After exploring the lifetime, we set about clearing those remnants of ill health, before moving on to the third relevant lifetime.

In her third experience, we uncovered yet another death related to the lungs and breathing. In this vision, Donna had been an older woman, when, at the time of her death, her lungs were attacked and her breathing stifled.

"My house is on fire, and I can't get out," she said. "I died of smoke inhalation in that house. I couldn't get my breath."

When she came out of her regression state, Donna reported that in her current life she had emphysema-like symptoms, and couldn't understand why because she didn't smoke and maintained a healthy lifestyle.

But after the session, her symptoms decreased measurably.

I had seen cases like Donna's before. Traditional medicine had found no problem, and although drugs had been prescribed, she was reluctant to take pills for a problem whose source was undiscovered.

While it's fantastic to be part of such a miraculous healing, it doesn't always happen in one session, as Kelly's case illustrated.

KELLY'S MIGRAINES

The severity of injuries that Kelly had sustained in eight car accidents within five years had resulted in migraine headaches, jaw aches, earaches, and pain in both her hip and neck. She also suffered from back pain.

The tall, lovely, and normally productive brunette had been unable to work for over three years and was involved in a lawsuit that threatened to stretch out for years to come. Kelly tried many alternative therapies for relief, and when I offered to help, she enthusiastically embraced the notion of looking into some past life trauma as one possible reason that she couldn't seem to get rid of migraine headaches no matter what kind of medical advice she followed.

She was a wonderful past life regression client because visualization and relaxed awareness came easily to her. When I started her session, I only knew that she had been in a couple of car accidents and suffered from migraines. She lay down on the bed, listening and relaxing as I dictated a guided meditation that took her to the distant past. Once she arrived at the scene of the first lifetime relevant to her head trauma, she answered questions I posed to her.

In the first series of visions, Kelly saw herself as a young man of

17. In her mind's eye, looking down at her feet, she saw work boots and discovered that the young man had died outside in the cold and snow. The feeling at the time of his death reminded her of a giant fist coming down on the top of his head, ripping it open. Then he felt his hip being torn off by some force coming from behind. Now detached from his body, he surveyed the scene from above, and saw that he had been attacked by a polar bear. He died soon afterward.

In the next scene, Kelly was a four-year-old girl, running and playing happily outside her home. She accidentally fell off a cliff, hitting the rocks in the ravine below with a strike to her temple. That blow occurred just before her neck snapped. The young child's body was not found for a few days.

The lifetimes kept coming as Kelly next saw herself as an Indian squaw in her 20s with a baby in a papoose fixed around the front of her body. On a beautiful day with a cool breeze blowing, she gathered wild berries for her tribe. From her new vantage point looking down on the scene, Kelly saw herself being stalked by a man in the woods. Her squaw-self was unaware of the man as he pulled back his bow and let an arrow fly. It pierced her cheek and exited her face just below her left ear. She died in the wilderness.

Searching for a motive, Kelly felt the man had killed her to take her baby, because his own wife was not able to bear children.

As the session continued, we discovered nearly a dozen lifetimes, each and every one ending with a head trauma:

• When she was a young man inside a cabin in the 1800s, seated in front of a cozy fireplace, a neighbor she'd had a minor dispute with burst in, crushing her skull with a rock. The blunt force trauma to the back of her head snapped her neck.

• In a scene where she was a soldier, the back of her head was beaten with the butt of a gun.

- In another traumatic death, she was sacrificed on an altar as a young infant boy when her father crushed her head with a rock.

In several other lifetimes, Kelly either broke her neck accidentally or someone else did it intentionally.

I hoped some of her head trauma would be relieved by all of these lifetimes we cleared, but in the following weeks, Kelly's head pain increased.

However, she was not deterred, feeling she was really on to something. About a month later, she returned for another session, discovering several more head trauma deaths:

- She was a young Indian maiden, about 14 years old, standing at the edge of a high cliff with a breathtaking view of the magnificent sea and scrub oak trees. The ledge gave way, and she fell a hundred feet down. She lay there with many broken bones and a head injury until her death a few hours later.

- On the open prairie, she was a 14-year-old boy, living in a sod house with her father. They grew a few crops to eat and sell. Because of this hard life, the father drank to dull the pain. One night the drunken man hit her in the head after an argument, killing her instantly.

- In another, fuzzier vision, her head was crushed under wheels, perhaps a vehicle or some kind of machinery, she said. Kelly felt the pain at her temples.

- And in the final vision, she was a 19-year-old Native American male hunting for shellfish when her leg became wedged underwater and she drowned. The last thing she saw was the face of some kind of sea creature she couldn't identify.

In this session, we released each of these traumas into the white light of the Holy Spirit, or we floated them away in pink balloons full of love, or we transformed them into new energies that would serve her instead of bringing her pain.

TRANSITIONS

Following these sessions, Kelly reported that she felt releasing these past traumas constituted a significant step forward. She now could consider resuming her career as a massage therapist, something she'd decided would be too strenuous with her injuries. Although she still had bouts of pain that sapped her energy, they were no longer daily occurrences.

But it would take more than just the release of these lifetimes to put the young mother back on the road to recovery. Other healers worked on her, too.

ENERGY WORK

Subsequently, Kelly told me she had been accepted into an advanced energy class, where the lessons began with students first working on themselves.

The initial class centered around repairing rips and tears in the energy grid around the human body, the foundation for clearing the energy centers, or "chakras." The teacher led her students in a regression, during which Kelly asked her guides to take her back to where she began to take on pain.

"It was 559 B.C.," Kelly said. "I was a kind of male witch doctor, and not a very nice one either. About 56 years old, I had just lost my only son to an epidemic. Even though I could heal many people of many ailments, I could not heal my own son, and I went insane. In my little hut, I saw a machete on the wall, and it gave me comfort. I killed everyone in the village as they slept, and my last thought before I passed over was 'I deserve to be alone. I deserve to suffer.'

"I treated these painful memories with Reiki [a healing laying on of hands], and as I came back to the present, a piercing pain I had carried through my body below my left breast and out my back was gone."

As Kelly continued to do class-assigned energy work on her own body through daily physical exercises, her healing progressed. Her dream of doing energy work is now realized, and the pain in her own body lessens each day.

Kelly's story is one of listening to your inner guidance, of persistence in the face of years of extremely trying circumstances, and of patiently waiting to see the positive results of negative events. Her positive attitude and courageous move toward a long-desired professional goal is inspiring to all who hear her story.

Past life regression is a useful tool for some people when it comes to dealing with persistent physical pain that's unrelieved by either Eastern or Western traditional medicine. I have also found it useful for unexplained attachments and irrational fears.

When both client and practitioner are aligned with God/Goddess/All That Is, and intend to proceed with a past life regression for the highest good of all concerned, healing miracles do happen.

WOMEN GATHERING TO HEAL

On a spectacular summer weekend, in the middle of the Olympic National Forest, the sisters of the sun, earth, moon, and stars came together in splendid harmony and love to honor Friendship in all its forms.

It was Womanfest 2004, and we met in a campsite along the north end of Lake Crescent. We banned brassieres, cooked and ate, and gave attention to our emotional, physical, intellectual, and spiritual bodies.

We were flashed by the radical Zelda, we were led in dance and song, we laughed, cried, rejoiced, and had our hearts touched to their deepest core. We pulled our emotions out of our chests and had a close look at them. We wished these healing moments could be offered to the men in our lives, and that they would find the same joy in them.

We confirmed the wide-ranging theories about women needing one another's alliances to be whole and healthy.

In one exercise, we thought of an international woman and sent her blessings and good wishes. We thought of whatever friend came to mind – Donna, Pat, Luisita, Heidi – and we spoke of how they had come into our lives, when, where, and what we appreciated about them.

Luisita, with her Latin ancestry that allowed for a free range of emotions, taught Diana how to emote.

Donna taught Suzie about integrity (and cheating at hopscotch).

When Amanda was a child, her friend Heidi taught her that other kids did not have it as easy as Amanda did by showing up at dinnertime – *very often* – to be fed by Amanda's family.

Pat taught Elisa that she was unique, and could accomplish anything.

"International Sister" was only one of the sharing games we played that brought us to tears and resurrected precious memories. We all felt grateful, and we put our collective gratitude into the middle of the circle and sent it out.

Meals were also special. They were lovingly prepared by our sisters who volunteered in the makeshift kitchen, and when we sat down together two or three times a day we were always able to get to know someone new.

The weekend was a wonderful time to commune with the Divine Feminine. I vow to do it whenever possible when women gather to heal one another.

SHAMANIC JOURNEYING

The last and best day I ever spent with my stepmother – a day cut short by Dad's anger – still weighed heavy on my mind months later, and I just couldn't seem to find my emotional footing.

I felt devastated that Dad had blown up the last physical chance Betty and I had at healing, and the loss of her was surprisingly profound. We hadn't had a lot of contact over the 40 years we knew one another, but I knew she was a communication portal to Dad and that the conduit was now closed. There would no longer be a translator/mediator between us and it wasn't going to be easy to have a relationship with Dad sans Betty. I was in deep grief and looking for a way out of it.

My spiritual education had been slowly but steadily turning in the direction of Shamanism for quite a while. Considered by many experts (including my mentor Penelope Smith) to be the best way to hone animal communication skills, it's a practice in which the animals play very important roles. Power animals, animal helpers and totems, and all manner of earth creatures offer wisdom on the Shamanic path. Like many indigenous peoples, we were learning to communicate with all life.

But I wasn't exactly after animal medicine this time. I had come to Port Townsend, Washington, to find my joyful self again through a Soul Retrieval with Shamanic healer Janet Goldenbogen Self.

Janet led me through the process using her skills to take the journey, see the visions, then reunite me with my lost soul parts by blowing them gently back into my body with her breath.

The journey revealed broken childhood selves, teenaged fragments, and adult pieces, all needing to find their way back to my fragmented soul. Each returning piece told Janet the story of its separation and each was relevant and revealing.

Some of the parts that I welcomed back included empowered silliness, an emerald green fairy self appearing as a regal Empress, a heart-centered worker, and multi-colored teenager pieces. Each of these disconnected pieces told Janet, then Janet told me, why they had detached and how to heal them. There were also helpers.

From the north, there came a menagerie of animals. Janet reported that these were animals I had helped already and who now had the strength to help me. The north also produced a representation of all of the animals I would help in the future.

From the east a flock of parrots came. First Janet saw one, then two, then thousands flew in. The parrot, a bird that can mimic human speech, is seen in Shamanic studies as a translator between humans and animals. We were definitely in my neighborhood.

From the south came meadow fairies specifically living under and around ferns. These were fern fairies, Janet said.

And from the west, the most beautiful breaching whale Janet had ever seen. "It is incredibly majestic and grand," she reported.

There were scenes from childhood where joy had been quashed, and there were scenes from teenage years pointing to the same thing. Thunder and lightning grumbled in its big bass voice, then clapped so loud it shattered old patterns, cracking the sky and letting in the light of transformation. "It's a symbol of a break with old patterns and the light shining through with new ways of being in the world," Janet explained.

I was tired and reflective at the end of the session, making my way out into nature for refreshment, then back home in silence.

After a nasty bout with a cold following the journey (which I considered a physical clearing), I definitely felt lighter and more joyful, accomplishing the goal of the session.

In a couple of business meetings, I noticed myself smiling broadly at nothing in particular. I also watched other people's reaction to me depending on whether I was smiling or not: an experiment with a predictable outcome, namely that people will react to you much more positively when you're smiling at them.

This magical soul retrieval helped the healing continue in earnest, and the deep gray clouds of grief and loss began to lift.

But there was still plenty more work to do, and joy would be found and lost and found again.

SEVEN

I CRIED A RIVER OVER YOU

I don't like you, but I love you –
Seems that I'm always thinkin' of you –
You treat me badly. I love you madly.
You've really got a hold on me.

~ Smokey Robinson

RUNNING OUT OF TIME

There is a March spring rain falling outside. I'm crying. I think I've cried almost every morning for the last two months. Today, I'm still crying about Dad, who inspires tears far too often. I've cried a river over that man.

Dad is over 80. We're running out of time. I know he's up and I know he's lonely. We could be bonding on the phone right now, but I hold back from calling. I'm just not strong enough to think about touching the hot stove this morning.

It's Sunday, so I also know Dad is most likely getting ready for his weekly Waffle Barn Restaurant trip with his son and granddaughter. I'm crying because I can't penetrate the wall of fear and call him. I'm crying because he's disappointed in me and because he doesn't really like me very much.

He loves me because he defines himself as a man who loves his children and I am his daughter. He loves me out of duty, which gives me the momentum to keep coming back.

But most of the time Dad is limited to two emotions when it comes to me: anger and disgust. Every now and then: annoyance. And there is also love. He's not afraid of the word, either written or spoken. It is spoken but not acted out.

The principles of intermittent reinforcement keep me coming back for more. Experiments prove that an animal who is rewarded intermittently will keep coming back for the reward with 10 times the intensity and frequency than an animal who is rewarded each time.

So I just keep pressing that lever to get a kernel of approval because every now and then one rolls out. Like a rat in an experiment, I'm never quite sure when the reward will be there, so I get bonked on the head countless times attempting to get it. But today, I don't have the strength to risk it, so I just cry instead. It's grievous.

Thank you Oprah, for giving us Iyanla Vanzant. Iyanla's show, "Iyanla Fix My Life," on your OWN network, along with Dr. Phil's program, have helped me on my path with Dad. I understand that as a child, Dad was not given what he needed to be a good parent to me. That's why he can't give me what I need from him. He doesn't have those tools in his emotional toolbox. Things like approval, kind words, nurturing, listening, and forgiveness.

His mother, taken by breast cancer when he was just nine years old, defined his life of lack. Because of his second wife, he was able to acquire some of these skills for the son they had together. But for me, he was stuck in a time warp when his first wife – my mother – had a tumultuous relationship with him, and then did the unforgivable: She left him. And when he sees me coming, all that nastiness is walking toward him. He's just plain mad, disappointed, and disgusted.

EMAILS

I email Dad. It's safer. He had an angry meltdown and declared he was finished with email and wouldn't be using it again.

I told him that email is a safe way for me to communicate with him "I'm sorry to hear that you won't be emailing anymore," I wrote. "It works well for me. I feel safer."

He was back to emailing within 24 hours. You've got to take Dad's declarations as mutable, and since I grew up in a house with completely different rules, it took me 50 years to figure out that Dad's MO was different.

In the household where I grew up, integrity meant you did what you said you were going to do. But in his house, you could completely change what you said you were going to do an hour later.

Growing up with two totally different sets of rules was always problematic in my relationship with Dad. At his house, I was always in trouble and usually puzzled as to why. At my house, I was praised as a good daughter getting good grades and following the rules.

In Dad's home, there was restraint and secrecy. From his early 30s and for the next 40 years, his wife lived with three males: her husband and two sons.

But in my house, five women-girls and a stepdad is how it always was. There was rarely a secret and no topic was off limits. The atmosphere was practically the polar opposite of Dad's house. There was hilarious bawdiness, innuendo, and openness as we talked about everything. Body parts and body functions were revealed, examined, researched, discussed, laughed about, and healed.

In a last-ditch effort to have a better relationship with Dad, I've asked if he will go to counseling with me. I know I have a snowball's chance in hell of making that happen, but I am now on a mission of avoiding regret. I don't feel I would have done everything I could possibly have done to have a better relationship with him if I don't ask before he's gone. Now he's 81. Tick, tick.

I float the email request out there and hold my breath. It still hurts when he is angry with me.

Taking the invitation as an opportunity to reflect on his lifelong experience with therapy, Dad writes back, saying:

> Betty [his wife] and I went to counseling for four or five days. When we left, I understood her feelings. I left the way I came. I would not hurt the one I loved by telling her how I felt.
>
> Our doctor once sent me to see a shrink too. I met him one time and scheduled another appointment for the next week. He killed himself two days later.
>
> I know your point of view already. Love, Dad

What an unfortunate turn of events. Allowing myself to indulge in *how it might have been* for a second, that shrink had an opportunity to change my life and he bailed out on it. Just think if the guy had continued to see Dad? He could have changed the family dynamic in a good way forever.

I knew I was in dangerous waters. Dad had tried to end the conversation about counseling twice already, so anger was undoubtedly building. But I soldiered on.

I countered:

> Hey Dad,
>
> Most people get into the field of psychology because they're trying to work some of their own stuff out. Some of the shrinks I've met and used were excellent at their jobs but their own home lives had a lot of issues in them. That didn't negate the fact that I always came away better; with more clarity and a deeper love for whoever I was trying to work through some issues with.

Improving our father/daughter relationship was a pursuit that required the greatest diligence in my life and my next answer to him was even more of my truth, as yet unsaid. I was pushing the envelope, and I knew it, yet I pressed on, trembling a little less, because I held out hope that we could have a conversation about something important to me that we disagreed on.

Dearest Dad,

Women work through things by talking. Men are usually less open to that. We are just brought up differently. Unfortunately we do not support men having feelings or expressing them in this culture. So they end up shooting their entire families instead of getting some help, or they have spurts of anger or other negative emotions erupting uncontrollably, or extreme reactions to small hurts. But I understand that many normal men just go to their man caves to process difficult emotions.

I am an advocate of mental health and it involves a great deal of courage to search for and express one's negative emotions. There is nothing you could say that would hurt me now any more than anything already done and said. I have also shared the most difficult stuff I have to share with you already.

So what I was seeing in asking you to go to counseling with me was a healing and a deepening of our love for one another. When people work through difficult emotions their relationships become closer and more loving on the other side of the work.

Dad, in the past I have shared my point of view on psychological matters and have been belittled for it. So please know that first, this is who I am according to my interests and my education. The way we tick emotionally is of great interest to me.

And secondly, this is a discussion. So if you continue to shut down my communications with statements like "I know your point of view already" you will get what you are asking for: very little sharing of my thoughts and views with you. And in my opinion, it is too late in your life not to open up the lines completely. So I continue to push for that. I love you, Dad.

He responded:

> I do not want to open wounds. Our relationship can be ongoing and you can believe whatever. But I know this: If your mother had wanted to have a home for her family I would have had it with her.
>
> Betty and I wanted you, and you wanted us. But your mother and stepfather refused to give you up. Betty was very hurt because you assured both of us that you wanted to live with us in Pedley.
>
> But when I took you home and asked your mother about it, your stepfather let me know that he and your mother knew better than me how to care for you. How he formed an opinion of me had to have come from lies your mother told him and told you also.
>
> I am not going to spend my last days fighting lies and ghosts. Please love me as I am or leave me alone.
>
> I truly do love you but since that day I knew if I was to have a chance with my new family I had to move north.
>
> To all my children: I love you as you are, please love me the same.
>
> I have had my nap. I rise early and have activity until lunch. After lunch I nap on the couch. Seems like I nap a little longer each day.
>
> I get disoriented easily. I am very nervous in unfamiliar places.
>
> Getting to this point has been good for me.
>
> Maybe we have turned a corner.
>
> I love you,
> xxoo Dad

Poor Dad. He always melted down into the time when, in his

mind, everything changed for him and me. When he asked if I wanted to come and live with him for my 6th grade school year and I didn't go. His wife was disappointed, and making her unhappy incurred his wrath on a greater scale.

I was 12. My stepdad, my Mom, and I sat down and talked about it, but since I came home crying and upset every single time I went to Dad's house to visit, we decided it was a really bad idea. But he was sure I didn't go because they had bad-mouthed him. He could never hear the truth of that situation, and I could not press his anger button with the truth.

I told him once and he heard, but it was almost too much for him because his beloved wife was so much at fault. It was painful for him to hear, and that was the same reason he wouldn't go to counseling. He was afraid of what I would have to say about her.

My complaints, in fact, were more about his not standing up for me when my stepmother was wrong in her treatment of me. It's always bothered me that Dad never had my back in those situations.

That's when I felt truly abandoned.

Now we were running out of time and I needed to know if more was even possible. Everything was getting more urgent. I searched for ways we could bridge the chasm between us before Dad left the physical world.

I pushed the envelope, then backed away, crossing my fingers and guarding my heart, and waiting for what would come next.

DAD'S TEMPORARY DEATH

Dad died today.

A huge team of swarming nurses brought him back. They were a very professional unit. Thank God they did, because Dad couldn't die. Seems like we had just begun a healing between us that wasn't even days old – more like hours, really.

These days I'm motivated by not wanting to have any regrets once Dad finds his way into the non-physical realms, and to be honest, I've believed for a long time that our communication would be better once he's on the other side. I imagined that maybe he could hear me better then.

But even though, as usual, I was nervous being with him, as soon as his failing body was breaking down seriously enough to put him into the hospital for open-heart surgery again in his 81st year, I got in my car and drove 6 hours north immediately.

We were good in the hospital about avoiding the hot-button issues. We discussed the weather, his beloved grandchildren, the nurses and hospital staff, and we watched baseball on the television until he faded off to sleep, when I would tentatively switch the channel to see shows like "Long Island Medium." Coming awake, he was puzzled by where the baseball game had gone and we switched back.

Uncharacteristically, Dad even made sure I had gas and parking money. His tender side was showing.

He was waiting on the side of his hospital bed when I first arrived, waiting in his hospital gown with ties in the back that were untied most of the time. The hospital, no place for resting, was fully staffed with nurses from Russia, Ukraine, the Philippines, India, and other exotic places. American nurses were few and far between.

But all of the health care professionals attended Dad well and constantly. Every half hour they had his cotton gown ripped open, pulled down or flapping in the wind. After a few days, poor Dad was completely frustrated at his loss of dignity, our constant questioning of how he was feeling and if we could do anything for him, and everyone's efforts to keep his gown together.

And he was in pain. The leg they had taken the vein out of for his earlier heart bypass gave him fits. One nurse reported that patients often told them that the chest pain was not as bad as the leg or groin pain after open-heart surgery. Dad said it felt like sciatica.

I coaxed Dad into a walk around the hall once, but the anti-skid socks he wore were loose and way too big. The toe end stuck out two inches and the socks stuck to the floor, essentially tripping him with every step. The socks supplied to every patient were a tripping hazard!

We were just waiting. Waiting for a place in the surgery schedule so we could move forward. It seemed like a long time and it was. Days.

Dad was the most restless man I knew, and waiting in a hospital bed was a challenge for him. The day he went into the hospital he'd been popping nitroglycerin pills on the golf course in the morning, but got no relief after about three pills. By the 4th hole, he was headed home not feeling well.

The ambulance took him to Kaiser, a huge hospital facility not more than 10 minutes from his house and one of the reasons he lived at Sun City, a golf retirement community in Roseville, California. Kaiser had been there for his beloved wife's illness and passing, and it was there for him now. He told everyone that he had no complaints about their care. Kaiser was one perk he negotiated for as a union rep all the years he worked at Pacific Bell and AT&T. Now all those years of work were paying off, at least in excellent, inexpensive medical care.

The nursing staff watched Dad as he waited. Every half hour they checked his blood-sugar level and his vital signs. The nurses and assistants fed him, medicated him, bathed him, humored him, and nurtured him. They finally removed his catheter after two days. There would still be nearly four more days of waiting, and the catheter, along with half a dozen other tubes, would make another appearance after surgery.

"I had a little trouble getting the equipment to work," he told me.

There were many visitors during these waiting days, but Dad wanted more.

"I'm so glad you're here. I was starting to get lonely," he told me one day, and I tried to take his comments personally. It was my second time at the hospital. I'd been there in the morning for a few hours and I'd reappeared around 6 p.m.

"I'm glad to be here, Dad. How long ago was it that you had a visitor?" I asked him.

"Oh, about a half hour, I guess," he said.

There had been at least six people there that same day. And now all the nurses on the floor were stopping to check in on one of their favorite patients. They laughed and joked with him and made him their temporary boyfriend. The man required a lot of attention. And he was getting it.

They EKG'd him, tested his blood, poked, prodded, inserted, removed, filled his veins with dye to find the blockage, and declared him pre-diabetic, with three vessels feeding blood to the heart blocked at the stents that were put in there 33 years earlier. He was a three-pack-a-day smoker then and had had the habit for 45 years.

"If it weren't for modern medicine, I wouldn't be here today," he told me.

Finally, a day later than expected, a bed became available at the heart hospital, and the ambulance crew came to take him 20 miles south to Sacramento's Mercy Hospital. My brother Sam followed the ambulance there, while I headed off to take care of some customer service issues. We both knew we had a couple of hours for catching up on work while he was settled into a new place.

Two and a half hours later, I joined Dad and Sam at the new hospital. Dad was scheduled for an 8 a.m. triple-bypass surgery the next day. We were all relieved to be moving forward.

POST-SURGERY

The next time I saw Dad he was in the recovery room all hooked up to every kind of device for measuring every bodily function possible. There was a stomach tube and a breathing tube – Dad couldn't breathe on his own yet. There was a three-tube hydra coming out of his chest for drainage. There was the catheter, and tubes in his leg also there for drainage from where the doctors had cut out the veins used to create the bypass for his blocked heart.

And there were needles connected to ports in his arms where medicines could be injected straight into his bloodstream. Half of his arm was bruised deep colors of red, purple, and blue. Half of his body was yellow from iodine washes of one kind or another.

I intended for Dad to hang in there. It was awkward when I first saw him. So much hurt between us and so many tears. In the past few months he had turned down all of my deepest and most heartfelt requests. I felt spent but I wanted him to know I loved him. I wanted to keep trying for something better than what we'd had.

Those were my reasons for being there for the surgery. And a text from Sam: "You should come. He wants you here."

Enough said.

Kids never give up on their parents if there's the slightest hope. And I still held that hope when Dad was at his most vulnerable and both of us were being reminded that time was of the essence.

TREADING LIGHTLY IN THE EMOTIONAL MINE FIELD

I love morphine. It's a fantastic drug I've never tried. But in my life, it has turned cruel people into caring people.

Dad had survived two open-heart surgeries at the age of 81, he was a little stronger every day, getting back to his old self, and I longed for the days when he was on morphine – those few precious days when he was kind to me.

My lessons were not over when it came to him. They were the most difficult lessons I have to learn in this lifetime. He taught me how to react to cruelty with kindness and love.

For the person taking morphine, there is painlessness, and then there are nasty nightmares, from what I hear. A little instant karma for all the meanness they've doled out, probably. I guess they're burning off a little karma before it builds up too much.

What must have Dad's young life been like for him to respond to kindness with cruelty? It must have been a nightmare.

Even as I cried crocodile tears, I reflected on all those women whose fathers completely abandoned them. My sister Becky is one of them. She offers me a completely different point of view.

Her philosophy: No dad is better than a mean or cruel dad. She thinks not knowing me and not living under the umbrella of my love is a great loss that my father chose. I think another great loss he chose was not knowing her.

Becky thinks she has it better than me since her angry and abusive dad was never really part of her life. Instead, she had a few step-dads who were kind to her. That works fine for her. She has also been in touch with the children her biological dad had with his next wife and they hate him for good reason. Children brought out his impatient, angry, and punitive side.

DAD MOVES

Late September. Dad has moved into his new assisted living apartment. They cook for him, clean for him, and every morning at 7 a.m. a man named Dick who Dad calls his shadow, arrives to make Dad's bed and hang around while he showers.

Dad sends me an email:

> It [healing] is going slow but steady. I am challenged daily. Please send me your phone number. I lost it.

But he never uses it again.

Then two days later he writes that he's getting the staples holding his heart in from his throat to his belly button taken out. It's got to be a relief.

He emails to a group of supporters, including me:

> I am getting stronger every day. Still no staying power. My cardiologist says it will be four to six months before my healing is complete. I do not think I will ever drive again. I mourn that. Sam and I are going to my old home this evening to take a last look at things I want to keep. Sometime in the future, maybe I will see you again. Love.

I try to comfort him with my response, holding my breath and double-checking that there isn't anything in my message that would make him mad. It's always a gamble with no guarantees, and Dad is given to floating emails out there so lots of people will respond with loving care. He's a very needy man.

Dear Dad,

It's hard to say from this vantage point as there is so much healing yet to be done. You may feel like driving in six months. I know for me driving would be one of the hardest things on earth to let go of, so I grieve for you and at the same time hold on to hope for you to be able to drive again.

Don't give up yet though. It's too early to tell!

Recovery can be so daunting, difficult and depressing. My heart goes out to you, Dad.

Love,
Suz

One of the great rifts I've had with my dad over the years is related to his wife Betty, my stepmother. We had a difficult relationship. I was a burden to her young family financially and the product of another woman who had hurt her husband.

My sister Janene, who is back in touch with Dad after 30 years, says he told her something that I want to correct. He said I wanted him to go to counseling with him because "she wants to tell me what a bitch Betty was to her." I want to set him straight because while that was truly a very painful relationship for me, I've come to resolution about it.

Once Betty got breast cancer, she was much nicer to me. And then there was the wonderful, happy, kind and charitable morphine day with her.

I call him up trembling and end the conversation with, "Dad, there is something I'd like you to know."

"What," he says.

"I did not hate Betty. I loved her," I say.

"Ok," he says, and we hang up.

In a subsequent email I take the risk to tell him again about the healing that took place between Betty and me. I'm not sure he believes me since he was so angry and distracted while I was there.

It was our last day together. Ms. Morphine was present. Betty and I sat close together on a two-person couch and looked at catalogs of clothes and she showed me some styles she liked. It was girl stuff. She told me, "I have always considered you my daughter too."

A slight gasp escaped me and I blurted, "That's the nicest thing you've ever said to me. Thank you."

It was the sweetest time. I tell Dad that story for the second time in my email, trying to get him to hear that we resolved many of our issues and were on good terms before she passed, his soulmate and his disenfranchised daughter.

> Good morning, Dad,
>
> I hope you are feeling better every day and that this will be a good day for you. I would like to come and visit you at your new place closer to the end of the month.
>
> What is your schedule right now? [We have both been very early risers in the past, but once I woke him up since his surgery and have regretted it.] Sleep is the best thing for healing so I don't want to wake you up. Have a good day, Dad.
>
> Love,
> Your first-born and Betty's only daughter (ha!)

Dad responds with a zinger that sets me back into an emotional puddle of tears for three days, writing:

> I am taking walks early, sitting out front and watching the day begin. Between 8 and 9 is a good time to call.
>
> Your reference to first-born has no bearing for me. My assets will be allocated as I see fit. Betty felt that a neighbor girl, Marsha, was her closest daughter. She looked up to Betty and they spent time doing things together.
>
> You spent most of your life with your mother and that is OK. You had many chances to live with us and heed my advice, but your stepfather, as you told me, was the major influence in your young life.
>
> My will is secure in my lawyer's safe and anything you might have seen at my house is not in my finished will.
>
> I had a great walk this morning
> Love, Dad

Why? Why? Why? Why would he want to deny the best day I had with Betty? Why would he want to hurt me so deeply? Is he just cruel? Or doesn't he get how devastating these words are to me? Or is he still stuck on proving I'm not okay since he didn't get to raise me? Why is he so resentful that my stepfathers were kind to me? One of the many things about me that makes him so angry.

I also realize that he has set me up. He had placed an outdated will right on top of his dresser drawer at home, in plain sight, so there was no possible way for me to miss its glaring presence when he asked me to bring him a pair of socks. I agonized over whether I should look at his will or not, then remembered an intuitive feeling I got from him when he directed me straight to the dresser drawer. I felt he wanted me to see it.

I crossed my fingers in hopes that it would not hurt too much, but it did. It had a history. An earlier will cut me out completely during the time he was the meanest to me. But in the current document, he was giving me a very meager percentage of his modest estate. It was truly a message of worth to me, and it hurt like hell.

Time out.

I set my intention to communicate from a loving place, and an emotionally mature heart that knows he is damaged beyond repair. He's attached to his wounds and won't give them up. And he has no interest in working through his pain or mine. I know I can only heal my own wound. Eventually, after crying my eyes out, I come to that place of love for him. My Guides are showing me his email with new eyes.

"He is showing you the places where he is in pain," they say. And looking again, I can see them. He gets angry when I say my stepfather was kind to me. He is angry when I try and find a place of tenderness with my stepmother's memory. He smashes these things in my face and sends me reeling with his message, but I can see *his* pain in it as I reflect on what happened to him when he was 25.

He fought for custody of me and his stepchildren, and was denied. In those days, fathers never got custody unless the mother was a complete basket case, and even then, it was rare.

But Dad asked his sister Mary to move in with him and she did: all the way from Georgia to California because his divorce attorney said that he had very little chance of getting custody of the kids, and if he didn't have a home and child care lined up, it would be impossible. So he arranged those things, and then he didn't get custody anyway, officially.

But Mother gave us to him for a few months. Having missed her salad days altogether, she dropped us off with different people for periods of time so she could be free for a short while. Dad loved children but Mother did not. She liked us much better once we were grown.

After a few months, my Aunt Mary decided she needed to go back to work. She was tired of living with her brother and caring for his kids while he went to work, and so we were all returned to Mom. She had secured a small apartment, new skills, and a new job by then, and was on the hunt for her next husband.

Dad's present-day words cut me deeply. I'm totally taken aback that he's talking about money and his will. It is painful that he can't hear the resolution I had with my stepmother and it hurts me deeply that he tells me no, she didn't consider me her daughter. They were the most nurturing and tender words I had ever heard from her and I was holding on tightly to them.

I cry, pray, meditate, and cry some more. For two days and two nights (a record short time) I process. "Do the work," I hear Iyanla Vanzant saying, and I'm doing the work of emotional clearing.

I will not answer Dad's email until I can answer from a place of love, a high calling. The work is grueling, exhausting, and yet so very worthwhile, because if I can get to unconditional love with this man, I can do anything.

On day four, I check in with my Higher Sources, getting the go-ahead to begin composing my email response.

Dear Dad,

It looks like I have hurt you with something I said about one of my stepfathers. I'm so sorry. No one could ever take your place. Please forgive me.

Betty and I worked through our difficulties and in the end we loved each other. She called me her daughter. I cherish that with all my heart.

> I am after your love, not your assets. I hope to find my place in your heart as your cherished daughter. I keep trying.
>
> I will always be the first-born child of Bill Vaughn and the last-born child of Janice McGahey.
>
> Love,
> Suzie

I do the visualization for detaching and letting go that I have given my clients time and again. It's very helpful. I hear my husband mirror my words back to me that I have told my clients a hundred times: Take nothing personally. Advice from Don Miguel Ruiz's book, *The Four Agreements*.

I meditate and pray that my email will be received with the love I surround it with. Then I click "Send" and hold my breath. If it can't be received that way, then I pray that I will be able to see any hurtful words coming back as a display of places where Dad was wounded.

Turning to my oracles, my direct link to my Higher Sources, I keep breathing. The rune stones bring a message from the Divine that says don't expect things to be different, just because you've had a breakthrough here. They send me Dr. Phil's words: "The best predictor of future behavior is past behavior." How I respond to any communication is up to me. I can only heal my own wound. So with Dr. Phil's words in my head, I check on what is likely to happen.

Dad will not respond to the email. He doesn't respond to positive missives. So most likely, he will send out a generic email to a large group of people, splattering cyberspace with a message to several female friends and relatives to see how much nurturing he can get back. It's all about getting sympathy and cyber hugs for the small wounded boy inside of him. And it's failsafe. I understand his little boy self is empty.

That's exactly what happens, so finally, I'm not disappointed. I have come to a new level of understanding and expectation. Misery is a result of not accepting the way things are, so my goal is to let go of the way things aren't. The email he sends to the group of women is already in my inbox by the next day.

He writes:

> It is 4 am and I am up. I have a few boxes of pictures to choose from to hang here at the apartment. I reach to pick up two or three at once, but I forget, they are heavy. The pictures pull me down into the box with them. Did I ask for divine help? No, I said *Oh shit* instead.
>
> A skinned elbow and a scratched arm. Lots of blood. Cleaned up now and Band-Aid in place.

I write back:

> Sorry about your fall, Dad. I hope you are not too sore today.

And leave it at that for now.

MEMORIES OF DAD'S LAST DAYS

Dad kept his wonderful sense of humor until the end of his life, joking with family members and ribbing the nurses and doctors at the hospital.

When he first met his urologist, he asked the young physician, "Are you a *real* doctor?" He laughed when he told me that story, saying Dr. Workman was at a loss for words.

When I visited Dad on Father's Day, he told me several stories and I interviewed him relentlessly whenever he would permit it. It was about a month before his passing.

He told me about Mabel, the wonderful black woman who cared for him and his siblings after his mother passed on when he was just 9 years old.

And he described union negotiations in San Francisco in the infant days of ORTT, when the union had a private meeting with management. Both sides were forced to listen to one another. Union leaders were upset that in the middle of negotiations for better wages and working conditions, the company put out a PR booklet titled "100 Ways to Make Great Hamburger Meals."

When it came time for the union leader to speak, the group was told that Brother Bill would take the floor. Dad read every word of that pamphlet to management. He said it took him a couple of hours because he took his sweet time. But the management team was forced to listen. He was just the rabble-rouser the union needed.

Dad said he felt as if he had no purpose now. I told him he was now supposed to tell stories and that's what I was there for, so he could tell me some.

LAST HOURS

A few weeks later, I got the call.

"Renal failure. Come up now if you can," Sam texted. That text would put me on the road to the hospital where I arrived about 11:30 p.m., relieving Sam of the first overnight duty.

By the next night we would switch that around so our 24-hour watch on Dad allowed Sam to go to work. I sat with Dad from 6 a.m. until 9 p.m., and Sam stayed overnight from 9 p.m. until 6 a.m. Time had little meaning except that it was fleeting, but for Dad, sleeping off and on, and waking off and on, it had nothing to do with daylight or darkness.

"Look who's here!" Sam announced to the half-asleep man on my arrival.

"Hi, Dad!" I said.

"Hi Suzie," he said with a half-sleepy smile.

Dad's first question to me was, "When do you have to leave?"

"I'll never leave you again in your lifetime," I told him, and I felt some of his anxiety dissipate with a heavy exhale as he nodded in understanding.

There were some tender times during the hospital days in the week before Dad died. I only saw his Angry-Bird look once: the brows pointing inward into a V-shape toward the bridge of his nose, shaking me to the core and sending me backing carefully out of the room. But I was leaving the hospital and the night crew in the form of Sam had arrived, so I was able to shake it off. Shaking off his anger was one of my greatest challenges.

On day three, I reached over to kiss his forehead good night and he drew away. Angry Bird showed himself. I moved in.

"Don't make me work for it, Dad," I told him.

Ben (his grandson) and I joked later about how he played hard to get sometimes, and later reflection told me that his show of anger meant he didn't want me to leave.

Another memorable interchange we had was during an Oakland A's baseball game. The game was on the TV and I sat quietly next to Dad as he slept and came in and out of awareness. It was only a few days before we took him home to hospice care.

"This is the first time we've been to a baseball game together, Dad," I told him.

"It is?" he asked, surprised.

"Yes," I said.

"I apologize for that," he said.

There were also a few serious times I tried to lighten up during the last week that Sam and I cared for him.

He was not a man who liked to be fussed over, and that was one of his last great challenges as we tried to make sure he was comfortable and pain-free. Nurses often asked him questions to assess his "mentation," or mental state.

"Bill? Bill?" they would ask until his eyes opened. "Do you know what day it is? Month? Who the president is? Do you know what you are doing here?"

Once when he was quite lucid, he said, "Yes. I'm playing left field for the New York Yankees." But often in the middle of the day, he would awaken from a deep sleep and tell me he didn't know where he was, asking, "When are we getting out of here?"

Sometimes he became annoyed and swung his legs over the side of the bed, ordering me to "get on the bus and let's go." He was always a restless man, never staying in one place for too long, avoiding crowds or groups, and making "drive-by" appearances at family functions.

"You can sit up but you can't really get up, Dad," I would say. "Your legs don't work too well."

He wanted to get up and take a shower but I had to remind him again about his legs. I helped him to sit up on the side of the bed, had him wrap his arms around me, but it only reinforced for him how weak his body really was, as he lay back down.

A parade of people passed through his hospital room. One was a young man who thanked him for helping him as a high school baseball player (Mike, brother of Matt), and many other young people offering thanks. Dad commented that it was pretty busy in there and I told him the throngs of people were letting him know how much he was loved.

Due to long nights of mouth breathing, Dad became thirsty. I (and the medical personnel) constantly asked him if we could get him a drink of water. Help was necessary since his arms twitched with involuntary muscle spasms as a result of the morphine and everything spilled when he held the cup. After many, many times of asking him if he wanted water one day, he finally said, "No, I can't take any more water. Niagara Falls is drying up."

I took advantage of him just a little. It was my opportunity to shower him with affection, which he resisted from me in his stronger days.

Once when he was half asleep, I put a thick layer of lipstick on and kissed him a dozen times all over the face until he woke for a minute to say, "Ok, that's enough." He couldn't protest the lipstick kisses and there were no mirrors in sight for him to protest the face painting. I smiled for a long time looking at it while he slept. I also took his hand and held it many times, and he let me do it in the end, without drawing it back.

There were a few minor battles. The underwear battle was one of them. Several times in his last few days he told me, "I need some underwear." With protruding tubes and poking doctors, his body was made accessible to all medical personnel and he lost any shred of modesty he ever had, but he still wanted underwear.

Once we were dispatched home from the hospital, I held up two kinds I found in his dresser drawer and asked what kind he wanted.

"Boxers or briefs?"

"Too many choices," he said.

I chose the green boxers and, ironically, I would be required to sign for those boxers when the Neptune Society took his body away. Loved ones have to sign for anything that's going out with the body and I whispered to him that the underwear he kept asking for would go to eternity with him.

Some of the last things he said were:

"I love you."

"I am not having any fun."

"I need some underwear."

"I want to take a shower."

"I want to talk to you."

"I'm miserable. Well, maybe I deserve a little misery."

"Forgive your old dad for being an asshole."

"I know you want to be first."

"Hi, Suzie."

"Water."

"Ice cream."

"This dying stuff is not as easy as I thought."

"I regret not being able to be civil to her [about my mother]."

Dad was given the option of staying alive a few months longer with the introduction of a kidney tube that would replace that non-functioning organ, but he declined any more invasive procedures. After the doctor explained the option again, he shook his head to say no, and repeated his decision several times.

After the doctor left the room he told me, "One option is living and one option is dying, and dying is what I want."

I know we will now have a chance to improve our relationship in the spiritual realms. He was one of my greatest teachers and our relationship taught me to choose unconditional love in the face of his difficult and often angry personality. I could not please the man due, in part, to his hatred for my mother and his inability to forgive her. I grieved at her loss too, as she wanted to be a comfort to him in his final days, but he would not allow it. He did not allow her name to be spoken.

Years of therapy helped me to see my father for who he really was: an injured child. It was a great opportunity to practice and to choose love no matter what he gave, and I held his hand with great tenderness as he passed from this world.

And holding his hand, I told him many times while he was conscious, semi-conscious, and unconscious, "Love is all that really matters, Dad." I had the opportunity to communicate with him telepathically during these times too and I could see he was moved by what I sent as silent tears rolled down his cheeks and he cried in his sleep.

I made it my mission to make sure he had the best care possible, worked on unconditionally loving him, and had no regrets. I loved him very much. Some of the things I loved about him were:

- His love of children

- His desire to do the right thing

- His fight for the underdog

- His grand sense of humor

- His devotion to Betty, his wife of 45 years

- His love of all of his ancestors and descendants

- His willingness to give California a try

- His work ethic

- His capacity to always say "I love you"

NORTH TO DAD'S MEMORIAL

In my early 40s I was teaching a media skills training course to employees of the state of California in the capital city of Sacramento. The gig was twice a year (until the state tightened her belt and closed down the State Training Center altogether).

This semi-annual trek showed me more about how I processed my relationship with my dad in the body because my body's reaction became so predictable.

In anticipation of seeing him, my lower back usually went out completely, I was bent over, and I had a hard time walking. There was definitely a hitch in my get-along.

Meanwhile, I was expected to teach a two-day course with a screaming pain going down my lower back and into my hips. It took me several years to put together that particular debilitating pain with going into my father's territory. But once I recognized the consistent pattern, I worked on clearing the body trauma preceding a trip to Northern California.

As late as 2013, when my brother Sam asked me to come and stay for a four-day weekend so he could get away with his girlfriend, I felt the pain and trauma. I was frightened about going but wanted to spend some time with Dad in his failing years. He was still recuperating from the tube they'd put in his bladder, a catheter the doctor announced would be permanent.

But the old fear returned to me, and before I left, my husband had to hold onto me while I sobbed for 15 minutes. He whispered that

I'd be all right, and then I dried my tears, got in the car, and drove.

I was always on edge, wondering how long Dad could be nice, or if he would crush me with unkind words, or maybe throw something across the room in a rage. There was blaming, belittling, and making fun of, in the early days, and a giant disconnect in later days, where he blew in, observed I was still alive and kicking, and wrapped up a quick drive-by visit when I was in the area staying at my brother's house.

I worked hard on letting go, and finding forgiveness and love in the face of what seemed like mostly anger, disgust, or lack of interest in my life. And there were vast swatches of personal landscapes that I had to be careful not to mention for fear of seeing the rage: namely the people and entities playing major roles in my life – my mother and sisters, my maternal family, and my businesses.

MY MOTHER: A FELLOW TRAVELER

So it was when Dad died that I asked Mom to accompany me to his memorial service in Northern California, the forbidden zone for her. She took the train seven hours north to my house, and I drove us north another six hours to get there. It was near Roseville: a place where she had never been allowed, a place where her name had scarcely been mentioned due to Dad's inability to forgive. She faced the peril of meeting with the angry disapproval of anyone Dad had spoken to about her, but she did it for me, and because I asked her to, never giving a second thought to which was more important. She was willing to walk through the fire if that's what was there.

The Blue Goose Events Center was the place we selected for Dad's friends and family to come and celebrate his life. On the walls were blown-up images commemorating his years as a young baseball pitcher; as the valedictorian of his ninth-grade class, when he was photographed in his spiffy rented suit; the time he put on a crazy clown hat and sat in a butterfly chair at the state fair for a photograph; and an old photo of days in the army, freezing in the snow in Bavaria.

The stage was decorated with the 60- by 40-inch oil portrait of himself and Betty he had requested. It was the same portrait that had taken center stage at Betty's memorial service when she passed. Neither of them had gray hair yet, so they were probably in their mid-40s.

At the service the army honored him with a bugler who played taps, and flags for Sam and me. Sam had selected those who would speak, including a favorite nephew, brothers-in-law, his best friend, his grandsons, his son, and finally me. He was remembered well, but what these people said was revealing. Their words gave me comfort that I was not the only one who found his personality difficult to handle.

Dad's brother-in-law, Keith, reported in his eulogy, "I used to introduce myself as Bill's brother-in-law and people would say, 'How do you stand that guy?' Then I figured out I should introduce myself by saying 'I'm Betty's brother.' Then they'd say, 'Oh we love her, she's great.'"

Dad's nephew hinted that even though Dad supported his daughter (Dad's goddaughter) by attending events like piano recitals, he didn't look very comfortable doing girl things. He felt much more at home on a baseball field throwing balls to the mitts of boys.

The memorial video was the concluding highlight to his service. I produced the loving tribute and found the perfect music for it. On screen, his life unfolds in a melancholy way as his mother dies, and we see five young children at her gravesite. Then the short six years when he was the father in my household with my mother and when I came along. The song "My Girl" introduces the next

40 years when he lived with and loved his soulmate, Betty. Finally, the video ends with the spiritual song "It Is Well With My Soul," as Dad grows angelic wings and takes flight from his rocking chair under a giant shade tree. "It is Well" is a song I began to hear hours after he passed away.

I recounted for the audience the best things about Dad I could muster up. One thing I remembered for them was a story he told me about the day his mother died and how a train whistle had blown just about the time she left her body. He'd told me that for the rest of his life, a train whistle reminded him of his dear mother. I knew he had joined her when, at the exact conclusion of the memorial video, a train pulled into the station behind the event center and blew it's whistle.

The service was warm, loving, and forgiving, and I set my intention for those feelings to anchor in my heart for my flawed father.

I thought about whether it was the right thing to ask my mother to accompany me to the memorial, and what Dad would have wanted. I have to believe that in the place where he was sorting out this life, all was forgiven, and as my brother said, speaking of Mom, "She took her rightful place at the service," telling her at the time, "You belong here."

There were several things that went into my decision to ask Mom to go with me, including the support she gave me all the years I tried to navigate the relationship with Dad. All during these years when the emotional abuse was severe, Mom always told me, "Your dad loves you. He just doesn't know how to show it. Hang in there."

And I would not cut him off, except to catch my breath and footing from a hard left hook. Some of the worst emotional punches took months of crying and hurt for me to find my way back to contacting him.

Another consideration was the support I felt I needed to get through the service. I wanted and needed someone in my corner. I had many folks there for me, but none with the same significance as my mother. Most of my life, I had faced the wolves alone. Now, I had my strongest supporter and my biggest fan at my side.

She alone knew what Dad could dish out because he treated us almost exactly the same. She propped me up through the most difficult relationship of my life, never wavering, and never speaking ill of him. She understood everything I was feeling, she felt the loss of what my dad and I could have had, and she felt the tears of the nine-year-old boy in Dad's memorial video as he stood at the graveside of his mother. She felt deeply for that little boy, and for her own daughter, and it brought her to tears.

Even though theirs was not a classic love story, Mom loved Dad for the child they made together. When they were young and starting out, she encouraged him to come to the Golden State, where he eventually *did* find his lifelong deep love in Betty, and Mom was happy for him.

But should I have taken her to a memorial service for a man who forbade the mention of her name? At the end of his life, Dad told me he regretted his inability to be civil to her. I decided finally that I might be helping him out spiritually by designating the memorial service as a way he could still accomplish that, and for a change, support me as well.

AKASHIC RECORD POST-MORTEM HEALING

Dad had been gone for about a month when I signed up for an Akashic Record Reading to help move the healing along a little faster. I had been waiting and watching for Dad to make contact through dreams, feelings, or visions, and it was not happening. As I tuned in to my Guides, I heard that Dad was in the midst of a long assessment mode and trying to figure out the lifetime he'd just left.

I contacted Janet Self, the same RN I'd worked with before. Janet has 30 years of experience in healing and uses her psychic gifts to view the records and also for Shamanic Journeying.

The first thing Janet told me was that Dad wanted me to know he was happy. I could see him surrounded by loved ones he had been missing terribly: his sisters Mary and Emily; his mother, Donia; his dad, Edgar; and others. Janet reported that he had put an angelic entity "out front" to speak for him while he prepared himself a bit better. This to me was evidence that it was really Dad. For most of my life he'd hidden behind my stepmother, and it was his MO to put someone out in front to deflect discomfort when topics became emotional.

But what was also like Dad is that it took about 30 seconds for him to throw the angelic entity aside and speak to me directly through Janet. That was just so like him too.

"He shows me a string on the ground," Janet reported. "You are on one end of the string and he is on the other. Neither of you are holding it. It's a message of missed connections. He says he just didn't know how to connect with you.

"He is showing me puzzle pieces now," she went on. "He's trying to fit them together to understand your relationship. A few are starting to fit together now that he has a greater vision from where he is now, but there are still several that don't fit. He's working on that."

Dad was an agnostic when he died and Janet brought that information through, saying he was spiritually empty. "He could have learned from you but he chose not to," she said. "He has a lot to learn before coming back."

Then Janet began to see a whole lot of blue. It was royal blue and Dad told her we were connected by blue. We have the same blue eyes, my dad and me, but this is also the chakra color of the throat, an area of my body needing healing as a result of Dad shutting me up and shutting me down.

I let Janet know I was available to heal that and would accept any assistance he could render from the other side.

As the Akashic Record Reading progressed, a huge parrot flew in to Janet's vision. She reported that it was a very large, colorful, and significant bird, making a dramatic entrance. This was another indication for me that we were in the right record because since parrots can mimic human speech they are regarded as ambassadors of the Bird Kingdom to the human kingdom. As a professional animal communicator, I felt it as quite a reassuring vision.

My difficult relationship with Dad as evidenced in my body by extreme sacral pain and sciatica whenever I made plans to visit him seemed to disconnect right around this time, and I felt two huge releases from that area of my body. The lack of discomfort was dramatic. I sent gratitude to all beings who helped with that transformation, and embraced a new lightness in my body.

Whenever I thought of Dad through tears of grief I sent him love. I had worked very hard to get to the unconditional part of it and now that he was non-physical it was more possible than ever for him to receive it, and easy for me to send it etherically.

Janet reported that Dad had not known how to love unconditionally. That he'd only known how to react with anger and resentment, and that he was learning, even now, about accepting the unconditional love I was still sending.

"Keep sending it," Janet advised. "As you do, more and more puzzle pieces fit together for him. He says when they all fit together he will find a way to let you know. I don't know what it is, but you will know.

"Your dad is tipping his cap to you," Janet added. "Is that a baseball cap?" she asked.

Baseball: That was Dad's sport. He was a pitcher who had once thrown a no-hitter and made the newspaper with his accomplishment in his small hometown.

But tipping his hat was far more significant than baseball to me. It meant he was finally a fan of mine too, and I cherish that image to this day.

EIGHT

FINDING MY JOY AGAIN

Walk as if you are kissing the Earth with your feet.

~ Thích Nhất Hạnh, *Peace Is Every Step:*
The Path of Mindfulness in Everyday Life

A COMMUNITY OF KINDNESS

It is 6 a.m. and my morning walk begins. Wintertime brings a mist to the air, the last remnant of a much-needed rain. Not exactly a storm, but here in dry California, we'll take an inch or two of measurable precipitation without complaint.

The birds are beginning to wake up but it's still dark on this quiet Sunday morning.

Saying hello and wishing the birds happy hunting for bugs and worms, as is my usual custom, I am delighted by the crows who walk with me, hopping and flying from roof to roof at the same pace as I move along on the ground.

Suddenly one of the birds flies down and touches my hair with her wings.

The bird-made flutter moves my hair like a light breeze, and as the air is displaced by the black span of feathers the sound it makes is distinctively strong and gentle at the same time.

Such an awesome event makes me feel privileged, and I go from smiling to shedding tears. I'm not quite sure why at first, so I allow the tears to move through to a clearer place before seeking the reason for them. 'What's up?' I ask my body. And gratitude for the work I do and the life I lead washes over me.

I am living in one of the most spectacular places on earth here on California's Central Coast. The only problem is that it's a little too far from the nurturing hugs of my mother and sisters.

But there is a light shining in an unlikely place: a car rental counter at the Santa Barbara airport. After missing the last flight of the day to San Luis Obispo from LAX, I stand at that counter to rent a car to drive myself an hour and a half north home.

That's where I meet Don. He is tired and asks me and my friend Judy if we'd like to share expenses and the driving since he's afraid he might fall asleep at the wheel.

"I missed the last flight too, so how about if we drive together?" he suggests.

He looks pretty safe and I'm not alone, so I say, "Sounds good to me."

Don Maruska is a great listener and a wonderful conversationalist. It turns out he's *The New York Times'* best-selling author of *Take Charge of Your Talent* and a former fan of mine from the old radio news and talk show days.

Eventually, our discussion turns to spiritual practices.

"I'm looking for a church where the women are allowed to be leaders," I tell Don.

"The church I go to has a lot of women in leadership roles," he says, offering a few more details about Saint Benedict's Episcopal Church in Los Osos, just northwest of San Luis on the coast. A few months later I find myself in the pews and under the spell of the talented priest, speaker, and nurturer, the Reverend Caroline J. Addington Hall, Ph.D.

It's not only Caroline Hall I've been led to, but an entire group of healing men and women who take me into their spiritual community. Even though I have no idea what their doctrine is, I don't care, and Rev. Hall doesn't seem to mind too much that I don't.

"I don't know what you believe and it really doesn't matter," I tell Rev. Hall. "I just want to be in a spiritual place where a group of people are focused on their Higher Sources."

"I hope you will find a comfortable place here in this spiritual community," she tells me.

And I do. The women, each with her own gifts, help me heal the grief and suffering of Dad as well as tough times in my personal life.

Rev. Hall offers a safe place to fall to pieces for about six months until I begin to glimpse my emotionally stable self in the mirror again. And her church is a place of serenity, communion, connection, and safety.

In addition, she offers a referral to a talented therapist, Jill Denton. And when my body starts to break down under stress, I'm thinking out loud about needing a good massage when Rev. Hall offers another referral to one of the best masseuses I've had in a long time, Cynthia McCabe.

My head, body, and heart are on the road to recovery in the tender care of these and several other women.

MY HEALING MOTHER AND MUSIC

Thank the Goddess for my mother who, with her wild and free sense of humor and silliness, can always lift me up. A hug, a kiss, a word of praise from her, or just holding her small hand is like a healing salve.

As my grieving begins to subside a bit, we take a 10-hour road trip, singing and laughing all the way.

Like Reba McEntire, I'm also healed by music when I'm on my own. Many an early morning finds me singing and crying until the tears are spent and the clearing is under way. Sad songs hold the words I want to express but can't, so I sing them to myself out loud, often in the car, and sometimes at the top of my lungs, pushing every ounce of angst out of my body through the tunes.

More healing women like Adele, k.d.lang, Susie Bogguss, Carole King, and Joni Mitchell sing the blues to me. And there are a few men too, like Jason Mraz, Bruno Mars, Dan Fogelberg, and a slew of Motown voices.

The priest with her kind concern, the therapist skilled in finding the way, the masseuse with her magic hands, the sister with her loving ear, women with adoring tongues, my mother tenderly sharing affection and music – all these women create a community of kindness that shows me the way to de-light on the other side of the tears of transformation.

I am grateful. Wait for me. I am making my way back. And in the final analysis, love *is* all that really matters.

EPILOGUE
Letter to a Young Suzan

Dear Suzie,

Inside your own life – as it is for Oprah behind her fame and influence – you are loved for your best qualities. But like Oprah – and many other women – you will be someone who will face numerous challenges to grow and to develop meaningful work, learning to communicate in mysterious and satisfying ways.

Your earliest memory will be revealed in a rebirthing session when you will uncover one of the themes of your life that will follow you until therapy unravels it.

You'll find yourself in the womb, anxious and impatient to get out. Then you'll experience yourself at the time of birth, shocked at the stark reality of the physical and thinking,' Wait just a minute. Is this what I wanted?' That experience will happen to you several times as your life unfolds.

One of the first decisions you'll remember making will be at the age of about 2 or 3 when your parents are fighting. In a regression you will see your diapered toddler self feeling distressed and reaching little hands up into the air, first for Mother, then for Father. Neither angry parent picks you up to reassure you, and you'll sit down hard on the floor.

Here, you'll make a decision not to need anyone else, and that resolve will follow you for quite a while as your life unfolds. Naturally, that won't work out too well and you'll be working on it for a few years in therapy until you fix that personality flaw. It'll be one of those lifelong works in progress.

You're a really smart kid and by the age of 4 you will have memorized several children's books, amazing some adults who will at first believe you've learned to read really early.

Know that once you turn 21, a boyfriend will begin to call you "Suzan" instead of "Suzie," influencing the rest of your life. Part of you will always be "Suzie" to those who have known you before age 18, so later, when someone calls you "Suzie," it'll be a cue that that person has been in your life a long time.

You suspect a lot of things that will, indeed, come true. Then you will examine whether those outcomes were premonitions or self-fulfilling prophecies, but you will likely never know.

Also be aware that the adults in your life now don't always know what they're talking about and you shouldn't believe everything they say.

There's one thing in particular you shouldn't believe now: that your looks are unacceptable and you need to lose weight. You're a perfectly normal-weight young person. The real truth is that you are small and athletic but the adults in your life don't see that. Try to ignore them when it comes to their judgments about your young body. You will look back on their films and photos and wonder why they were already bribing you to lose weight when you didn't need to. It will turn out to be a self-fulfilling prophecy, providing you with a lifelong struggle.

You are a wise child. That's why people are already relying on you as if you were a parent sometimes. You may be surprised to learn now that you really do know some of the things you think you know. Other issues will unfold like a favorite multi-colored star lily.

You'll find success in academics, and with praise from teachers and administrators you'll be reluctant to leave school. Partly, you'll be afraid you're not capable of making much money. There will be many people standing in line to get your first broadcasting job for very little pay and it'll be a struggle. But eventually you'll select a career out of love for the work and prove your innermost beliefs true.

You'll stay in school for an extra degree because you know for sure that you're good at being a student. You'll consider going back for a doctorate for only one reason: Mom wants you to have that personalized license plate reading "Dr. Suz." But the challenges you face as you make your way through a master's thesis may haunt you and your M.A. may be as far as you go.

Yet you'll always be the kind of person to identify a

fear and go straight for it, to clear it out.

You will work on your relationship with your dad for many, many years, even when he's gone from this world. This work will reflect your desire to accept all of his limitations and to gain freedom from needing him to be someone different than who he is. He will be one of your greatest teachers but growth will come through pain and a river of tears. Keep remembering he's doing a lot better than his own parents did. Your mother will keep reminding you that he loves you but doesn't know how to express that.

You'll continue to work on rejection and self-acceptance throughout your life, and you'll find that contentment is what you can really get in this life, not prolonged ecstatic happiness, although moments of that will surface. The goal is to move into the center of the wheel of life so as to keep from spinning out on the edge, so wildly happy and wildly depressed are to be avoided.

Even now, in your young years, you have very little drive to be a mother. Some people will tell you you'll regret that and you'll sense that they are talking about themselves. That's also true. You will never regret your decision, and just like you thought, you will have many children in the form of clients and that will work out just fine. You will also be able to choose fostering if you get the itch to dedicate every fiber of your being to guiding another human on their way, but for you that would be a big stretch.

In your 20s you will live near the ocean with a bunch of unkind roommates, and after that short stay wonder if you will ever have a home with an ocean view again. As I write this to my young self from my 58-year-old self, and from a place that is far from an ocean view, I wonder the same thing again. But I'm going to say yes to you, and it'll happen in your 50s.

Your life path is one of communication and counsel. You will speak to great leaders, animals, trees, and even insects, bridging the gap between nature and humanity. You already love the way the tongue makes different sounds with different languages from different ethnic groups, and your lifelong friends will come from around the globe.

As a true Sagittarian, you'll have your suitcases standing ready and your traveling shoes well worn, and you'll learn diplomacy from teenage rejection due to your sign's brutal frankness. You'll never tolerate dishonesty and won't commit easily, but once committed you'll be in for the long haul.

You will also discover that love is not all there is to compatibility and a long-term relationship - you can have love and little else. Autonomy, freedom, and mobility will be critical to your happiness.

In the middle of your life you will change careers completely, bruising your ego for a while, and you'll struggle to find yourself professionally again. But you will succeed, developing new passions in your work life, and nature will play a central role in a bright new second-half-of-life chapter that will unfold in unexpected ways. Your spirit animal, a baby coyote by the name of Yip, will lead you to embrace the fun and joy of your new career in animal communication, and will try to show you how to lighten up on the heavy responsibility you've always felt to do your best work.

You will be a spiritual warrior, the one whose battle is the self with the Self. Your great love for all sentient life will be rewarded in great and small ways.

It's a good time to start now to learn to nurture yourself. When you feel criticized, imagine that all those around you are giving praise instead. Let's reverse this trend early.

All of your three stepfathers, and the other significant men in your mother's life whom she doesn't marry, will think you are a great kid/teenager/person and it will help somewhat with the fact that your biological dad does not much like you.

And P.S.: Your favorite stepfather will be your mom's sixth husband. Wait for it.

Love,
Suzan

ACKNOWLEDGMENTS

My thanks and gratitude go to all the women who have nurtured me on my journey, several named in the section "Finding My Joy Again." My mother and my sisters top the list of female support that has always been there for me.

Thank you, Mom, for lending a non-judgmental ear, and for being the one I could speak to in whatever way I needed to at the time: with anger, sadness, frustration, profanity, love, or compassion. You held my sentiments tenderly. You've always offered me a shoulder and a soft place to fall, and I am so thankful to have a mother like you.

Gratitude goes to my sister Terrie, who, like every first-born child, dealt with young and inexperienced parents, often focused on their own needs at the expense of their baby girl. Mom practiced on you and my other siblings, honing her skills to a high degree before she got to me. Thank you for taking the heat and for your love.

I am thankful for my sister Janene, who has always loved me and wanted the best for me. Please know I am glad you had a chance to give and receive love from my dad (your favorite stepdad) once again at the sunset of his life. I am particularly happy you were able to experience father-love from a man, who, unlike your own biological father, wanted to love you instead of hurt you.

To my sister Becky, who has always been one of my biggest fans and who is always in my heart, I also give thanks. She's the sister who is there in a New York second if I need anything, and who hears my confessions with an open heart and mind, only occasionally raising an eyebrow (usually in curiosity). I am so grateful that you always see the best in me, reframing and renaming what I am in loving ways. Thank you for seeing me as a comforter and a professional when it comes to my work with animals. I love you the Bess.

I am grateful to my editor, Vicki Hanson, who can always make a book out of a bunch of stories. She's the best person I know to slog through the mud of words in an attempt to uncover the story trying to be told. I'm so glad I have this kind of collaboration with an editor who's got my back. Thank you, my friend.

And I thank my Dad, who at this very moment is tipping his baseball cap to me from Heaven in a gesture that says, "Yes, I see you and I am now a fan of yours, my precious daughter, my first-born child." I'm sending you love on your continuing journey, Dad.

www.ingramcontent.com/pod-product-compliance
Lightning Source LLC
Chambersburg PA
CBHW052006090426
42741CB00008B/1578